CONTENTS

—

CONFESSION

HOLY COMMUNION

"Mother Loyola has won enviable distinction as a writer of books which treat of the spiritual life. Her mind is vigorous, her heart is large, her information is accurate, her style is refined and vivid, and her pen is easy—all these qualities combine to give her works a high rank in Catholic devotional literature. Few writers in English have fathomed as she has fathomed the depth of the treasures contained in the Holy Eucharist and the solemn preparation that should be made for a worthy reception of our Lord in Holy Communion....To help us speak this "welcome" reverently and heartfully, tenderly and fervently, is the object of this exquisite book which is full of vigorous thought and of sturdy emotion. It will always be a most acceptable gift to devout souls, but, above all, to those who are serving God in the sanctuary of religion."

—from a review of *Welcome!* in Donahoe's Magazine,
November 1904.

And the spirit and the bride say: Come. And he that heareth,
let him say: Come. And he that thirsteth, let him come:
and he that will, let him take the water of life, freely. (Apoc. 22:17.)

CONFESSION
AND
COMMUNION

*For Religious and for Those
Who Communicate Frequently*

BY

MOTHER MARY LOYOLA

EDITED BY
REV. HERBERT THURSTON, S.J.

2021
ST. AUGUSTINE ACADEMY PRESS
HOMER GLEN, ILLINOIS

Nihil Obstat:
SYDNEY F. SMITH, S.J.

Imprimatur:
HERBERTUS CARD. VAUGHAN,
Archiep. Westmonast.

This book was originally published in 1898
by Burns & Oates.
This edition ©2021 by St. Augustine Academy Press.
Editing by Lisa Bergman.

ISBN: 978-1-936639-37-3

Unless otherwise noted, all illustrations in this book,
including the cover, are public domain images.

TO THE

FATHER OF OUR LORD JESUS CHRIST,

OF WHOM ALL PATERNITY

IN HEAVEN AND EARTH

IS NAMED.

PREFACE

THERE are moods and seasons with nearly all of us, when the use of some manual of devotion in our preparation for Confession or Holy Communion is recognized not merely as a help but almost as a necessity. No doubt our best prayers are those which are said in our own words, and which are merely the outpourings of a heart already filled to overflowing. Both in the flood-tide of consolation and in the desolate forlornness of any grievous spiritual trial, the worshipper prostrate before the Blessed Sacrament is in no humour to avail himself of set forms of words. In the one case his whole soul is ringing with a canticle of praise and thanksgiving; in the other he can only reiterate that exceeding bitter cry for which our Blessed Saviour in His Passion has given us both the example and the warrant. But between these two extremes there are many intermediate states. There are hours of spiritual aridity and there are hours of physical lassitude. There are times when we are worried or distracted, or, it may be, tempted; and there are occasions when we feel the danger of falling victims to routine, and when a temporary change of method seems desirable, if only for variety's sake. Under such circumstances, spiritual writers recommend that even those who normally and on principle accustom themselves to speak to God like children in their own simple language, should try to rouse themselves from their lethargy by adopting for a while the words and ideas of a printed book of devotion.

It seems obvious that, for such a purpose, the brighter and fresher the thoughts to which we turn as a corrective to our own dulness the better. There is, generally, no great relief from monotony to be found in our old-fashioned prayer-books, and in many of the devotional manuals translated from foreign languages, there is often so much which irritates and palls that the book proves a distraction rather than a help. The prayers which are printed in this little collection of suggestions are all original, and they have the charm of simplicity and of a certain directness of language which many will find helpful. Those who are acquainted with the author's previous book, called *First Communion*, and with the short collection of prayers for First Communicants which accompanied it, will probably give a very hearty welcome to any other contribution from the same pen. Although these "suggestions by way of preparation and thanksgiving" are intended primarily for the use of Religious, it is thought that they may perhaps be found useful by other pious souls who are in the habit of communicating frequently.

In a few words of preface contributed to the book just referred to, I was asked to make some reference to the practice therein followed of using *You* for *Thou* in addressing Almighty God. The same peculiarity will be noticed in the pages which follow. The practice has so far escaped any pronounced censure, and there is no doubt much to be said for the author's view that a certain stiffness and formality attaches to the use of *Thou*, which seems especially out of place on occasions when we wish a child-like affection to be the dominant motive in our prayers.

It need only be added that most of the stanzas of hymns and of translations of hymns occasionally introduced in this little book have been taken from collections in common use, excepting that a few verses of the *Adoro Te devote* have been borrowed from an unpublished version by a Jesuit Father.

HERBERT THURSTON, S.J.

CONFESSION

SUGGESTIONS

BY WAY OF

PREPARATION FOR CONFESSION[1]

I.

PRAYER FOR LIGHT AND HELP

O Lord, my God, I come to You once more for the forgiveness of my sins, my many sins. I come to You in this sacrament of mercy for that forgiveness which is the fruit of Your great mercy. The deepest need of my soul, the need that is ever deepening as life goes on, is union with You, my God—that there should be nothing between You and me. Only my sins, and the consequences of my sins, hinder this union, and so You call me to You again and again, that You may wash me yet more from my iniquity and cleanse me from

---

1 N.B.—It is by no means supposed that all the matter will be used each time. Much is offered that there may be room for choice and variety.

my sin. *Cor mundum crea in me, Deus*[1]—Create a clean heart in me, O God!

Cleanness of heart is my best preparation for Holy Communion, it is the one disposition You require. Finding it when You come to me, Your Real Presence will produce all its blessed fruits, and by a close union here prepare me for a union hereafter that will satisfy even the boundless craving for You that You have put into my soul. And therefore, again and again, I say to You, *Cor mundum crea in me, Deus*—Create a clean heart in me, O God!

Father, glorify Thy name.[2] Glorify in me the power of the Precious Blood. It would be a great glory to You to make anything *of me*. Sometimes we hold up a work for admiration, saying, "See!—and that was made out of nothing." So let me glorify You one day, my patient God. You have begun a good work in me; it concerns You more than me that it should be completed. Reward Yourself for all the labour and disappointment I have caused You. Bring me up to Your ideal. You can, and You have the will. Show me some day to Your Heavenly Court, and say, "Behold the work of My hands, brought at last to this—not only out of nothing, but in spite of frailty and opposition and sinfulness of every kind!"

---

1   Psalm 50.   2   John 12.

Your design in this sacrament is to give me not only the forgiveness of my sins, but also the most powerful means, next to the Holy Eucharist, for attaining to the perfection at which by my vocation I am bound to aim.

Self-knowledge and humility, strength and courage, peace, progress, and earnest perseverance in Your service—all these are its fruits, all these I shall receive in proportion to the dispositions I bring. Help me, then, to improve my dispositions each time I approach it.

Before the words of absolution, I shall hear other words, in which the priest in Your name frees me from all censures. *In quantum possum et tu indiges.*[1] Ah, Lord, if only You would say those words to me in another sense. If You would promise me grace in this sacrament to be measured only by Your omnipotent generosity and by my need, *"as far as I can and thou needest it."* You alone know the amount of grace to which these words would entitle me, the demand on Your Divine treasury for which You must be prepared if my need is to be met. And do You stint me? Do You put any limit to the grace I may receive? None. What You look for chiefly is desire. *"He that thirsteth,* let him come, and *he that will,* let him take the water of life freely."[2] Your holy servant the Cure d'Ars bids us, when we go to pray, open our hearts as the fish opens its mouth

1   As far as I can and thou needest it.   2   Apoc. 22.

when it sees the wave coming. Much more do You bid us enlarge our hearts when we draw near to Your magnificent sacraments. *Open thy mouth wide and I will fill it.*[1] *If any man thirst let him come to Me and drink.*[2] *If thou didst know the gift of God, . . . thou perhaps would have asked of Him, and He would have given thee living water.*[3] My God, could You press us more earnestly to ask for what You are so ready to give? I do know, in part at least, this gift of God. I ask, and with all the earnestness of my soul, for this living water. And ask that I may thirst for it ever more and more, as I come hither to draw. So shall I glorify Your mercy, so shall I fulfill Your designs, so shall I magnify the power of the Precious Blood.

And now, my God, I take up the easy part You assign me, in the great work we are to do together. Help me with Your grace throughout. Enlighten my mind, and inflame and strengthen my will. And first enlighten my mind. Show me my soul as I shall see it in that day when You will *search Jerusalem with lamps*,[4] as I shall see it in the hour of my Particular Judgment. It is not the faults of mere frailty that will affright me then, but the deliberate opposition to Your will, deliberate infidelity to grace, deliberate meanness in my dealings with You.

---

1   Psalm 53.   2   John 7.   3   John 4.

4   Soph. 1.

Faults of surprise in which my will had little share do not estrange me from You. It is *my will* You look at. It is the *acts of my will* I have to examine—the voluntary carelessness in Your service, the willful transgressions of Your law laid down for me in Your Commandments, in my Vows, in my Rules. What have You thought of the past week, my God—of my relations with You, with my Superiors, with my equals? What should I have ready at once for Confession, if You were to show Yourself to me now and bid me kneel down for absolution? This I will take to Your feet, of this I will accuse myself, on this shall my purpose of amendment fall—the rest I need not mind. Two or three faults in which there was wilfulness, and perhaps some shabbiness with You that will help me to a blush—this with a sin of my past life, for which I renew my sorrow, will be abundant matter for loving self-accusation, loving sorrow, loving purpose of amendment for the future.

> *Veni, Sancte Spiritus,*
> *Et emitte cœlitus*
> *Lucis Tuæ radium.*
>
> *Veni, Pater pauperum,*
> *Veni, dator munerum,*
> *Veni, lumen cordium.*
>
> *O Lux beatissima,*
> *Reple cordis intima,*
> *Tuorum fidelium.*

Holy Spirit, Lord of Light!
From Thy clear celestial height
Thy pure beaming radiance give!

Come, Thou Father of the poor!
Come, with treasures that endure!
Come, Thou Life of all that live!

Light immortal! Light Divine!
Visit Thou these hearts of Thine,
And our inmost being fill.

II.

EXAMINATION OF CONSCIENCE

(N.B.— We have all our own method of examination of conscience, and a glance will often give the history of the week. To some, however, the following hints may be of use.)

1. Towards God

1. *Confession.* What did You think, my God, of my last Confession? Not what did *I feel*, but what did *You* think of its sincerity, its humility—above all, of the care to weigh the motives for contrition and of my purpose of amendment?

2. And my *Communions:* what have You thought about them? Not what have I felt. What about preparation—remote and immediate? What about the observance of the Additions, which secure the first and last thoughts of the day for God? Might not greater fidelity as to these make all the difference in my Communions?

3. *Mass.* How do I hear it? What union with the priest in offering this sacrifice and mine? . . . What union with our Lord? . . . What remembrance of the Passion? . . . Of the four ends of sacrifice? . . . What prayer for the living and the dead? . . .

4. *Meditation.* Not how has it succeeded, but what has been my preparation—remote and immediate? . . . observance of the Additions? . . . Do I take pains to have the matter clear? . . . to spend most time in colloquy? . . . to make my prayer practical? . . . In the Reflection to examine my meditation carefully, with a view to amendment? . . .

5. *Examination of Conscience.*

(a) *General.* Do I give most time by far to the motives of sorrow? . . . Do I try to elicit at least two intense acts of perfect contrition every day? . . .

(b) *Particular.* What care and earnestness in making and marking ?

6. *Office.* Fervour kept up by intentions for different hours? . . . By renewal at *Gloria Patri?* . . .

7. *Morning and Night Prayers. Visits to the Blessed Sacrament. Rosary. Angelus. Grace.* Do I at least make a good start, recalling presence of God: "Where am I going, and for what?" . . .

8. *Presence of God* recalled during the day? . . . *Ejaculations?* . . . *Intention* renewed frequently? . . .

Outward acts of reverence, e.g., genuflection, taking holy water? . . . What about *fidelity to inspirations?. . .*

9. *Spiritual Reading:* with prayer for grace, application of mind, and the effort for perfection? . . .

10. *The Vows.* Poverty: Any carelessness as to giving, taking, lending, borrowing, without leave? . . . Any laxity in presuming leave? . . . wasting?

Obedience: Prompt, cheerful? . . .

2. My Neighbour

1. Superiors: reverence and love? . . .

2. Equals: at recreation? at work? . . . Charity in thought, word, and deed?

3. Inferiors: charity? prayer for them? prudence in commanding, firmness in exacting, in all things kindness? . . . Is there carelessness, indolence, selfishness?

3. Myself

Humility? Custody of the senses? Regular observance, particularly regarding punctuality and silence? . . . What about my predominant passion and the faults into which it has led me? . . .

Household work, in spirit of humility, diligence, devotion? . . .

Throughout my examination noting, not feelings, not repugnance, but the part my will has played, *i.e.,* deliberate acts of choice.

A FULLER FORM OF
EXAMINATION OF CONSCIENCE

1. Towards God

1. *Sacraments.* Regularity. Do I postpone? and if so, why?

(a) *Confession.* What did You think, my God, of my last confession? Not what did *I feel*, but what did You think of its sincerity, its humility—above all, of the care to weigh the motives for contrition and of my purpose of amendment?

(b) And my *Communions:* What have You thought about them? not what have I felt? What about preparation, remote and immediate? Do I make the usual acts before and after?

2. *Rising.* Prompt, at a fixed time? First thoughts given to God? Morning Prayers before leaving room?

3. *Daily Mass, Meditation, Spiritual Reading.* What about these acts which the Catechism names first and foremost in "The Christian's Daily Exercise"? I note the word "Christian," not Religious, "Daily," not by

fits and starts, and "Exercise," implying effort, self-denial, a good start at least, patience with weariness and distraction, perseverance.

(a) *Mass.* How do I hear it? What union with the priest in offering his sacrifice and mine? What union with our Lord? What remembrance of the Passion? Of the four ends of sacrifice? What prayer for the living and the dead?

(b) *Meditation.* Do I take pains to have the matter clear? to spend most time in colloquy? to make my prayer practical?

(c) *Spiritual Reading*, with prayer for grace, application of mind, and desire to profit?

4. *Church Services, Sermons, &c.* Am I late, or inattentive? Am I reverent before the Blessed Sacrament? *Visits to Blessed Sacrament.* Do I make it worth our Lord's while to remain in the tabernacle for me? *Rosary, Angelus, Grace.* What fidelity and earnestness? Presence of God recalled always before prayer?

5. *Night Prayers.* With what fervour as the last act of the day? Do I ever make pleasure or late hours an excuse for omitting them? What about family prayers? If impracticable, is the fault mine?

6. *Examination of Conscience.*

(a) *General.* Do I give most time by far to the motives of sorrow? Do I try to elicit at least one intense act of perfect contrition every day?

(b) *Particular*. What care and earnestness in making and marking?

Is my piety guarded by common sense and charity? Does it help or harm those of my household? Do I, under pretext of piety, neglect the duties of my state of life?

2. Towards my Neighbour

1. (a) Do I often remember our Lord's words: *"Judge not"*? Do I watch over my likes and dislikes—study tact and patience with those I dislike or with those who dislike me?

(b) Have I disedified any one by word or conduct? Is any one the worse this week for having met me? Do I avoid scandal as I would the pest? Do I join or willingly listen to uncharitable conversation? Am I careful to protect the good name of the absent, and do I remember that it is of precept to make restitution when it has suffered by my calumny or detraction? What about criticizing? sharp words? resentments? How do I make or receive an apology?

(c) Am I on my guard against subtle forms of jealousy? Does it vex me that good work should be done by others and not by me? Am I readily aggrieved because others seem more considered than I am?

Will my ordinary conversation bear examination? Is there any one who could reproach me with unkindness this week? Am I silent about complaints which my friends have confided to me? or have I been the cause of misunderstanding?

(d) Do I reverence priests, remembering that they handle the body of the Lord? Am I careful not to injure them or their ministry by criticizing or inconsiderate words? Do I embarrass them by being indiscreetly devoted to one particular priest or Order to the exclusion of others? With regard to my confessor, am I careful to avoid speaking to others of what may be said to me in confession? Do I remember that what may be good advice for me, may be very bad advice for them? Do I refrain from remarking upon the confessions of others, the time they may take, or the confessors they frequent, remembering that this is no concern of mine, and a matter in which curiosity is most reprehensible?

Am I considerate of the time of priests, and am I willing to believe that others' spiritual needs may be more pressing than my own?

(e) Am I a supporter of good works, or do I cry down any? Do I remember, by alms, the interests of souls, by helping missions at home or abroad, schools, &c.?

Have I injured tradespeople by speaking disparagingly of them without sufficient reason? Have the poor cause to complain of me for injustice, harshness, or neglecting them, like Dives? Am I prompt in paying wages and debts?

What do I do to help the struggling poor, the sick, the unsuccessful? Am I easily discouraged in my good works, giving them up through pique, jealousy, inconstancy? Do I try to spread the faith, and seize chances of learning how to explain my faith and answer objections?

2. If I am in authority:

(a) Have I looked well to the ways of my house?[1] Do I remember that I can delegate, but never abdicate my authority, and never divest myself of my personal responsibility in the government of my household?

(b) Do I show reverence, submission, and love where I am bound to show it? What about self-sacrifice and forbearance? What about anger, irritability, sharp words, selfishness? Am I considerate of the time of others, of those who are busier than myself?

(c) Do I guard my children as the apple of my eye— try to make the practice of religion sweet to them— insist on habits of obedience, regularity, and industry? Am I doing my best for my children, either personally or through others? Do I look upon their training as

---

1   Prov. 31.

the gravest of my responsibilities and the dearest of my privileges? Does my influence and example arouse in them the love of God and hatred of sin? Do they learn of me unworldliness, a loyal love of holy Church, and self-sacrifice in the interests of souls? Am I as anxious that they should grow up staunch and fervent Catholics as that they should get on in the world? Do I know what they read, and prevent or promptly stop dangerous reading? Am I firm in not allowing sons or daughters to keep late hours? Do I err by overstrictness or by over-indulgence? In any risk of damaging the innocence of children, do I remember Christ's words about the mill-stone? Am I careful never to be an occasion of sin to a child? Do I pray for all those whom God has given me?

(d) The welfare of my servants. Do I see to it?—that they are sufficiently instructed—that they have time for their religious duties? Do I treat them with kindness and consideration?

3. *If I am under authority:*

How do I treat parents or those in authority over me? As I should wish to be treated, were I in their place? What about disobedience, disrespect, provoking them, causing them anxiety, rejecting reproof or advice? Do I waste or injure what is theirs? Waste time which I owe to them? Am I impertinent or discouraged when told of my faults? Am I obstinate in following my own will?

3. Towards Myself

Have I an order of the day, and do I keep to it?

Do I waste time? If so, how?

Do I read novels without advice, and am I moderate even with good novels?

Have pleasure and self-gratification a secondary place in my life, or do I make them my occupation? Do I give way to sloth of mind or body, frittering away my hours or my days?

Do I know my predominant passion? Into what sin does it lead me? What efforts am I making to overcome it?

Do I courageously try to root out pride and anger?

Does my Good Angel note in me vanity in toilette, dress, talk? Does he see frivolity, curiosity, unfeminine self-assertion, or independence?

Do I shun amusements or occasions that I know to be dangerous to me? Do I guard my senses in order to guard my heart?

(Throughout my examination noting, not feelings, not repugnances, but the part *my will* has played, *i.e.*, deliberate acts of choice.)

III.

CONTRITION

It belongs to You, my God, to give me the sorrow which without Your help I cannot have. Will You refuse it? No father will give his child a stone if he asks for bread, or a serpent if he asks for a fish. If we then, being evil, know how to give good gifts to our children, how much more will You, our Father in Heaven, give good things to them that ask You. Give me, my Heavenly Father, what I ask. Give me "what I desire—an interior knowledge of my sins and an abhorrence of them." Give me "shame and confusion, give me great and intense grief and tears " on account of my many sins.

It belongs to You to give me what I desire; but it belongs to me to show I desire it, to weigh the motives, to be sorry *because* of the punishment my sins have deserved, *because* of "Christ in torments and death" for my sins, *because* of the outrage to Your infinite goodness by my sins.

1. Hell

If I have ever committed a mortal sin, I may go down to the gates of Hell, and looking through the bars of the prison-house, see what that sin has done. The moment I sinned, a place was prepared for me there. I may imagine that my name was written over it, and that the devils as they passed it knew it as mine. Let me see it and its surroundings. Above it Heaven, from which I was shut out. Below the horrors of the bottomless pit. On every side the sights and sounds of that *land where no order but everlasting horror dwelleth,*[1] the devils, and all that is most loathsome in human wickedness. And infinitely worse than all the torments awaiting me from without, the agony of remorse, the maddening despair, the loss of God which in itself is Hell. All this prepared for me. All this prepared by me, my own deliberate choice when I chose to separate myself from God. For God is all good. There can be no good apart from Him. He cannot make good apart from Himself. If we will not have Him, we cast away all good. In rejecting Him, I tore myself away from everlasting joy and gladness, from consolation, and peace, and security, and light, and love. What is there left for the lost, for those who have lost God, but darkness and destruction, everlasting misery and despair?

---

1   Job 10.

It is from this that the patience of God has saved me. It waited and bore with me, and at length won me and saved me. I am here still with my chance of Heaven. I may say, "My God, I am sorry," for He is *my* God still. I may look up and say, "Our Father, Who art in Heaven."

It was for me, *for me* that the patience of God provided the Sacrament of Penance. *Know you not that the benignity of God calleth you to penance?*[1] O patience of my Creator, I grieve from the bottom of my heart for having sinned against You so sorely. I thank You for saving me from the punishment my sins deserve, for making even the prison-house of Hell a point from which I may spring up to my God and be forgiven and taken back to His Heart. If ever "through my fault I should forget His love, at least let the fear of punishment keep me from falling into sin."

2. Heaven

If I have ever offended God by grievous sin, I may go up to Heaven and, looking through its golden gates, see what my sin has lost. There amid the many mansions of my Father's House is one prepared from all eternity for me. On the day of my baptism it was

---

1   Romans 2.

set apart for me, my name was written over it, and angels and saints as they passed to and fro knew it as mine. To secure it for me, the providence of God has ordered all the events of my life, and all His wisdom has been employed in furnishing it for me.

On every side are the joys and delights which eye hath not seen, nor ear heard, nor the heart of man conceived; the rejoicing throngs of the saints; the blessed company of the angels. Above, Mary, Queen and Mother, in all her glorious beauty. Higher still, the Sacred Humanity—"the Lamp of the Heavenly Jerusalem." And over all the *Fountain of Life*,[1] the Blessed Trinity, Father, Son, and Holy Ghost, the unveiled Face of God. All this mine, offered to me, prepared for me. All this deliberately thrown away by me—for what? And the patience of God bearing with me, waiting for me, offering me His Kingdom again and again, as often as I chose to accept it. O my God, I fall on my face before You. I grieve from the bottom of my heart for the sins by which I have lost the place in Your Kingdom You have prepared for me, by which I have lost You and the eternity I was to spend with You, before Your unveiled Face.

---

1   Psalm 35.

3. The Passion

The sight of Hell and the sight of Heaven can show me something of what sin is, but not as the Passion shows it. They move me to contrition, but not as the Passion moves. Let me go to Gethsemane, or to the column of the Scourging, or to Calvary, if I would learn the hatefulness of sin and the patience of God, and so be led to a true and tender contrition.

A. GETHSEMANE

In the dark Garden let me see,
    Beneath the olives' moon-pierced shade,
My God alone, outstretched and bruised,
    And bleeding on the earth He made.

And let me feel it was my sin,
    As though no other sin there were,
That was for Him Who bears the world,
    A load that He could scarcely bear.

O Jesus, when my heart is hard and sorrow comes but slowly, let me find my way over the brook Kedron, up the slope of Olivet into the lonely Garden of the Agony, and there learn what the sins of my life and the absolutions of my life have cost You.

God has always required for forgiveness of sin, contrition, confession, and satisfaction.

In the Garden I see our Lord as the Model of penitents. I hear His cry of sorrow, *My Soul is sorrowful even unto death.*[1] I hear His confession when, recognizing in Himself the likeness of sin and the victim of the Father's anger, He cries out in His fear, *If it be possible, let this chalice pass from Me.*[2] I see His satisfaction in the sweat of Blood which His interior conflict draws from His sacred body.

> O Soul of Jesus, sick to death,
>   Thy Blood and prayer together plead,
> My sins have bowed Thee to the earth,
>   As the storm bows the feeble reed.

I grieve for my sins, for all my sins. I grieve for that drop in Your cup of agony which was my contribution to the Passion.

B. The Prætorium

Let me go down the slope of Olivet and cross Kedron once more, and taking my course northward enter the Pretorium of Pilate, and fling myself on my face before the column of the flagellation. Let me hear the sound of the whizzing scourge, weighted with my sins. Let me lie there till the five thousand stripes have paid the price of my absolutions, and I may go away

---

1   Mark 14.   2   Matt. 26.

free, leaving Him on the pavement in a pool of the Precious Blood. Ah, Lord, shall I not at least leave my heart with You—not broken by sorrow as I should wish, but still truly penitent—the contrite and humble heart that You will not despise!

c. Calvary

It was long ago, two thousand years nearly. But there was a day and an hour when a cross was raised outside Jerusalem, with One nailed upon it to die a malefactor's death. Let me take my crucifix in my hand and consider attentively what a death that was. Has ever malefactor suffered more than He? Think of the scourging that went before; think of the crown of thorns; look at Him now, nailed to the cross—the living Flesh nailed—hands and feet nailed by the huge spikes driven through them into the wood. The gentlest handling of those wounds would be agony, and He has to hang upon them with the whole weight of His body for three hours—until death.

Look at Him—see the tortured head; the dull, glazed eyes; the parched lips; the quivering limbs; the ever-widening wounds. Think of the intense thirst; the dislocated bones; the agony of every nerve and muscle. Could I look unmoved upon the worst of malefactors in such a pitiable plight?

And is He a malefactor? No.

Why, then, is He here? For me—in my place—to suffer the pains due to my sins. He is here, hanging on the cross, to teach me what sin is—what sin deserves—to what my sins have brought Him. If ever I have committed one mortal sin, I have had a distinct share in bringing about this death of pain and shame. See how uncomplainingly He suffers in every member of His body, in every faculty of His soul. See how the Divinity withdraws Its support from the Humanity except to enable It to suffer more. See how willingly He endures all this—*for me*, to atone for my sins, to satisfy the Father for me, to win me the absolutions of my life.

O Jesus, I fall on my face before Your cross to ask for an "intimate knowledge of the hatefulness of sin," to ask for grief, tears, and a sense of pain in union with You in torment, debased thus in order to die for my sins.

Can I doubt that the fruit of Your Passion will be the full remission of all my sins, that if they *be as scarlet they will be made as white as snow*?[1] He that spared not even His own Son, but delivered Him up for us all, how will He not also with Him give us all things— give me His forgiveness and His peace?

---

1   Isaias 1.

D. The Prayer in the Garden

He fell upon His face, praying. (Matt. 26.)

He fell flat on the ground and He prayed. (Mark 14.)

I look at the tabernacle. He is there, Who on a night long ago lay prostrate on the ground in the Garden of the Agony.

The Joy of Heaven and earth in agony! Why, Lord? And He tells me why:

I fell down before the Lord for all your sins which you had committed against the Lord and had provoked Him to wrath. For I feared His indignation and anger wherewith being moved against you, He would have destroyed you. . . . I lay prostrate before the Lord. . . . I humbly besought Him that He would not destroy you. . . . And the Lord heard Me and would not destroy thee.[1]

O all-prevailing Prayer of my Saviour, I bless you, I thank you, I put my trust in you. What else did you win for me, O Divine Prayer, or rather by what means did you win for me that *Mercy of God* through which I am *not consumed?* By winning for me the grace of contrition for the sins which have provoked the wrath and indignation of my God. Give me, O Lord, give me now the fruit of that Prayer. Give me a deep, tender, hearty contrition for my sins—all my sins, for everything great and small

---

1   Deut. 9.

by which I have angered, and grieved, and disappointed the Lord my God, Who even when I offended Him bore with me, and waited for me, and would not destroy me—because of my Saviour's Prayer.

E. Popule Meus!

If the Jews had had a spark of generosity in them, they must have been moved by the touching words of Moses when, with his great disappointment fresh upon him, he made his last appeal to them in sight of the Land of Promise, *the goodly land*,[1] which he was not to enter, because—he gives them the reason: *He hath been angry with me on your account.*[2]

He was on the borders of that Land to which all his desires had tended, towards which he had patiently guided his stiffnecked people for the space of forty years, in which he expected to see them established: *I besought the Lord, saying, Lord God, Thou hast begun to show unto Thy servant Thy greatness and most mighty hand. . . . I will pass over, therefore, and will see this excellent land beyond the Jordan, and this goodly mountain and Libanus. And the Lord was angry with me on your account, and heard me not, but said to me: It is enough: speak no more to Me of this matter. Thou shalt not pass the Jordan, . . . neither shalt thou go in thither.*[3]

---

1   Deut. 4.   2   Deut. 4.   3   Deut. 3.

His hope cut short by a word. The desire of his life denied him just as it seemed to be realized. Punishment when he looked for reward. This, then, was the recompense his people had brought to him, *their leader and their prince*,[1] *the lover of his brethren*,[2] *who had stood in the sight of God to speak good for them and to turn away His indignation from them*.[3] And there is no word of remonstrance, no repining, only that gentle reminder: *The Lord was angry with me on your account.*

Popule Meus!—I kneel under the cross and look up. I look upon that *worm and no man, the reproach of men and the outcast of the people*.[4] I see the thorn-crowned head drooping on the breast—the hands, and feet dug through—the parched tongue—the cheeks wet with mingled blood and tears. *The whole head is sick and the whole Heart is sad. From the sole of the foot to the top of His head there is no soundness therein: wounds and bruises and swelling sores*.[5]

Why, Lord? The answer comes from the dry, pale lips: *The Lord was angry with me on your account.* On my account. "*Hæc omnia propter me.*" For me the thorns and the nails, the vinegar and the gall, the wounds and bruises and swelling sores. All this for me.

---

1 Jerem. 30.   2 2 Mach. 15.   3 Jerem. 18.
4 Psalm 21.   5 Isaias 1.

I pass within the veil and tremblingly I look into that soul. I see its anguish—the disappointment of its unrequited love—the darkness of its dereliction. I hear its desolate cry: *My God, My God, why hast Thou forsaken Me?* [1]

Why, Lord? *The Lord was angry with me on your account.* "*Hæc omnia propter me.*" All this *for me.* He loved me and delivered Himself *for me.* I look upon Him Whom I have pierced—on Whom my iniquity has been laid—by Whose bruises I am healed. O Jesus! and I find it hard to be sorry for my sins. Take away my stony heart and give me a *heart of flesh,* [2] that I may turn at last to Him Who has loved me even to the death of the cross—turn to Him, and cleave to Him with all my heart and soul and mind and strength, that *neither death nor life, nor things present nor things to come, nor any other creature shall be able to separate me from the love of God which is in Christ Jesus, my Lord.* [3]

4. The Patience of God

Patient and of much compassion. (Exodus 34.)

You are called, my God, *a strong and faithful God, keeping His covenant and mercy to them that love Him and that keep His commandments, . . . and repaying forthwith*

---

1 Matt. 27.   2 Ezech. 36.   3 Romans 8.

them that hate Him, so as to destroy them, without further delay, immediately rendering to them what they deserve.[1]

Why, then, have You been so patient *with me?* Why has there been so much delay and no rendering at all to me what I deserve? O strong and faithful God, if I had loved You always as You deserve to be loved, if I had kept Your commandments faithfully, could You have shown Yourself more faithful than You have? Can I find it in my heart to grieve You always? Can I hold out to the end against You, O strong and faithful Lover of my soul?

5. God infinitely good

We cannot understand what sin is because we cannot understand what God is. And yet the attribute of God which sin outrages most directly is the one that impresses us more than any other—His holiness. We fear it more than we fear His wisdom, His power, or even His justice.

It was the holiness of God from which Adam and Eve sought to hide themselves, "amidst the trees of Paradise," after their sin.

If when our Lord came amongst us the little children swarmed around Him, and publicans and sinners pressed

---

1   Deut. 7.

upon Him, so that their company was made a reproach against Him, it was because He veiled His holiness. When for an instant He let its presence be felt, all men quailed before it. Peter felt it after the miraculous draught of fishes. It was the holiness rather than the power of our Lord that impressed him and made him fall at Jesus' knees and cry out: *Depart from me, for I am a sinful man, O Lord.*[1] The Centurion felt it when he said, *Lord, I am not worthy that Thou shouldst come under my roof, say but the word and my servant shall be healed.*[2] The soldiers and the priests felt it in the Garden, when they went back and fell to the ground. At the Last Day it will be the holiness of God that will terrify the wicked and make them cry to the mountains and rocks to fall upon them and hide them *from the wrath of the Lamb*. The angels are not pure in His sight. Before His throne the eternal song is *Holy, Holy, Holy,*[3] as they cover their faces with their wings.

O holiness of God, I fall on my face before You, to ask for contrition for my sins. *Have mercy on me according to Thy great mercy.*[4] O God, be merciful to me, a sinner.[5]

---

1   Luke 5.   2   Matt. 8.   3   Apoc. 4.

4   Psalm 50.   5   Luke 18.

Which of Your Divine perfections, I wonder, will most overwhelm me when I stand before You, my God, the first moment after death? Will it be Your holiness? Will it be Your wisdom or Your justice, Your beauty or Your sweetness or Your love? All these will penetrate me through and through. But, oh, I think it will be Your patience, the patience that has borne with me all my life through, which will so stir my soul to its depths that but for its immortality it would sob itself away at Your feet. There will be no want of contrition then. Oh, that the contrition of that hour might be mine now!

And thus by hell, by Heaven, by Olivet, by Calvary, by the heights of Your ever-blessed perfections, I climb to You, my God.

IV.

FIRM PURPOSE OF AMENDMENT

What must You be in Yourself! What must be the overflowing goodness of that Nature which can spend itself on one like me! Shall I not love it for its own sake!

O God, all good, the only good, surely the proof of Your infinite goodness is found in this—that You are good *to me*. You must be infinitely good to be good *to me*. O goodness of God which I have outraged, O patience of God which I have tried so sorely, I grieve from the bottom of my heart that I have ever offended You, I grieve for the sins of the past week, for the sins of my past life, especially for . . . And I purpose, with the help of Your grace, to labour with new courage at the work of my salvation and perfection, particularly by the avoidance of this fault, . . . and by attention to my Particular Examination.

Et dixi, Nunc cœpi.[1] Now do I begin. "Help me, O Lord God, in my good resolution and in Your holy service, and give me grace now this day perfectly to begin, for all I have hitherto done is nothing."

---

1   Psalm 76.

V.

THANKSGIVING

Salvation to our God, Who sitteth upon the throne, and to the Lamb.[1]

Benediction and glory and wisdom and thanksgiving, honour and power, and strength to our God for ever and ever. Amen.[2]

Great and wonderful are Thy works, O Lord God Almighty; just and true are Thy ways, O King of ages.[3]

Salvation and glory and power is to our God. Alleluia.[4]

Give praise to our God, all ye His servants: and you that fear Him, little and great.[5]

O give thanks to the Lord, because He is good; because His mercy endureth for ever and ever.[6]

Let them say so that have been redeemed by the Lord, whom He hath redeemed from the hand of the enemy.[7]

O all ye Religious, bless the Lord: praise Him and give Him thanks, because His mercy endureth for ever and ever.[8]

---

1   Apoc. 7.   2   Apoc. 7.   3   Apoc. 15.

4   Apoc. 19.   5   Apoc. 19.   6   Daniel 3.

7   Psalm 106.   8   Daniel 3.

Sanctus, Sanctus, Sanctus Dominus Deus noster
omnipotens: qui est, et qui erat, et qui venturus est.
Et laudemus, et superexaltemus eum in sæcula.

Dignus es, Domine Deus noster, accipere laudem, et
gloriam, et honorem, et benedictionem.
Et laudemus, et superexaltemus eum in sæcula.

Dignus est Agnus, qui occisus est, accipere virtutem:
et divinitatem, et sapientiam, et fortitudinem, et
honorem, et gloriam, et benedictionem.
Et laudemus, et superexaltemus eum in sæcula.

Benedicamus Patrem, et Filium cum Sancto Spiritu.
Et laudemus, et superexaltemus eum in sæcula.

Laudem dicite Deo omnes servi ejus, et qui timetis
Deum pusilli, et magni.
Et laudemus, et superexaltemus eum in sæcula.

Laudent illum gloriosum cœli, et terra; et omnis
creatura: quæ in cœlo est, et super terram, et subtus
terram, mare, et terra, et omnia, quæ in eis sunt.
Et laudemus, et superexaltemus eum in sæcula.

Gloria Patri, et Filio, et Spiritui Sancto.
Et laudemus, et superexaltemus eum in sæcula.

Sicut erat in principio, et nunc, et semper, et in sæcula
sæculorum. Amen.
Et laudemus, et superexaltemus eum in sæcula.

Oremus.

Omnipotens, sanctissime, altissime, et summe Deus, summum bonum, omnem bonum, totum bonum, qui solus es bonus, Tibi reddamus omnem laudem, omnem gloriam, omnem honorem, omnem benedictionem: et omnia bona Tibi referamus semper. Amen.

or,

Hymn to the Precious Blood

Hail, Jesus! hail, Who for my sake
Sweet Blood from Mary's veins didst take
    And shed it all for me;
Oh, blessed be my Saviour's Blood,
My life, my light, my only good,
    To all eternity.

To endless ages let us praise
The Precious Blood, Whose price could raise
    The world from wrath and sin;
Whose streams our inward thirst appease,
And heal the sinner's worst disease,
    If he but bathe therein.

O sweetest Blood, that can implore
Pardon of God, and Heaven restore,
    The Heaven which sin had lost:

While Abel's blood for vengeance pleads,
What Jesus shed still intercedes
    For those who wrong Him most.

Oh, to be sprinkled from the wells
Of Christ's own sacred Blood excels
    Earth's best and highest bliss:
The ministers of wrath Divine
Hurt not the happy hearts that shine
    With those red drops of His!

Ah! there is joy amid the saints,
And Hell's despairing courage faints
    When this sweet song we raise:
Oh, louder then, and louder still,
Earth with one mighty chorus fill,
    The Precious Blood to praise!

                  (Indul. ioo days.)

My God, I believe most firmly in the efficacy of Your sacrament which I have just received. I believe that You have washed me from my iniquity and cleansed me from my sin; that as far as the east is from the west, so far have You removed my iniquity from me.

I know, my God, that I am wanting in confidence in You. I know You say to me time after time, *O thou of little faith!*[1] Yet see how I come to You week after week

---

1   Matt. 14.

for my absolution. Is there any want of trust here? Is there the least misgiving as to Your forgiveness? Can You not say to me at least after confession, *Great is thy faith!*[1] I desire to glorify You greatly by my faith.

My God, I trust You, I trust You with all my soul. Oh, it is easy to trust You after confession! I trust to You my past, my present, my future. I trust to You my soul, my body, my life and my death, my trials, my temptations, my salvation, my eternity—and had I anything more, dear Father, or more precious, I would trust it all to You. I desire to glorify You exceedingly by my trust.

My God, I love You. I love You with all my heart and soul and mind and strength. *My God! My God!* Oh, blessed thought, that in spite of all the past, You are still my God. Be mine always, intimately mine, and I ask for nothing more in time or in eternity. *For what have I in Heaven, and besides Thee what do I desire upon earth? . . . Thou art the God of my heart and the God that is my portion for ever!*[2] I desire to glorify You above all by my love. And in the spirit of love I renew my vows.

Eternal Father, I offer You, together with my vow of Poverty, my soul with all its powers, beseeching You to give me strength from Your omnipotence to resist all things that are contrary to Your praise, reverence, and

---

1 Matt. 15. 2 Psalm 72.

service, and to dispose of me in all things according to Your will. *Sume, Domine, et suscipe!*

Eternal Son, I offer to You, together with my vow of Chastity, my body with all its senses, beseeching You of Your unsearchable wisdom to give me prudence, to detect and avoid whatever may offend Your pure eyes, and to dispose of me in all things according to Your will. *Sume, Domine, et suscipe!*

Eternal Spirit, I offer You, together with my vow of Obedience, my heart with all its affections, beseeching You of Your overflowing goodness to give me grace to cleave to You with such constant fidelity that I may never in any the least point swerve from Your guidance—and to dispose of me in all things according to Your will. *Sume, Domine, et suscipe!*

"Eternal Lord of all things, I make my oblation with Thy favour and help, in presence of Thine infinite goodness, and in presence of Thy glorious Mother, and of all the saints of the Heavenly Court."

You promise me a hundred-fold, my God, for offering You my vows, would that I could offer You a hundred-fold for accepting them!

(BEFORE OR AFTER)

Litany for Confession

Lord have mercy on us.
Christ have mercy on us.
Lord have mercy on us.

God the Father of Heaven,
God the Son, Redeemer of the world,
God the Holy Ghost,
Holy Trinity, one God,

Jesus, Who didst come to seek and to save that which was lost,[1]
Jesus, Who art not come to call the just, but sinners,[2]
Jesus, Who willest not the death of a sinner,[3]
Jesus, Who when we repent rememberest our sins no more,[4]
Jesus, Who dost call to Thee all who labour and are burdened,[5]
Jesus, Who hast said "they that are in health need not a physician, but they that are sick,"[6]
Good Shepherd, Who hast given Thy life for Thy sheep,[7]
Good Shepherd, Who, having found the sheep that was lost, doth lay it upon Thy shoulders rejoicing,[8]

Have mercy on us.

1	Luke 19.	2	Matt. 9.	3	Ezech. 18.
4	Jerem. 31.	5	Matt. 11.	6	Matt. 9.
7	John 10.	8	Luke 15.			

Good Samaritan, binding up our wounds and
   pouring in oil and wine,[1]

Jesus, Who hast borne our infirmities and carried our
   sorrows,[2]

Jesus, Who wast wounded for our iniquities and
   bruised for our sins,[3]

Jesus, by Whose bruises we are healed,[4]

Jesus, Who art indeed the Saviour of the world,[5]

Jesus, Who, being now lifted up, wilt draw all things
   to Thyself,[6]

Jesus, Who hast promised that him that cometh to
   Thee, Thou wilt not cast out,[7]

Jesus, Who hast reconciled all things unto Thyself,
   making peace through the Blood of Thy Cross,[8]

Jesus, Who didst die for all, and hast given Thyself a
   redemption for all,[9]

Jesus, Who didst love me and deliver Thyself for me,[10]

Jesus, Who hast blotted out the handwriting that was
   against us,[11]

Jesus, Who hast taken it out of the way, fastening it
   to the Cross,[12]

Have mercy on us.

1	Luke 10.	2	Isaias 53.	3	Isaias 53.
4	Isaias 53.	5	John 4.	6	John 12.
7	John 6.	8	Coloss. 1.	9	2 Cor. 5.
10	Galat. 2.	11	Coloss. 2.	12	Coloss. 2.

Jesus, with Whom there is mercy and plentiful
  redemption,[1]

Jesus, merciful and faithful High Priest, Who hast
  compassion on our infirmities,[2]

Jesus, of Whose fullness we all have received,[3]

Jesus, Who art not ashamed to call us brethren,[4]

Jesus, Who wouldst be made in all things like unto
  Thy brethren,[5]

Jesus, Friend that lovest at all times,[6]

Jesus, more friendly than a brother,[7]

Jesus, Who hast loved us with an everlasting love,[8]

Jesus, merciful and patient, of much compassion, and true,[9]

Jesus, Who when we were yet a great way off, running
  to us, didst fall upon our neck and kiss us,[10]

Jesus, weeping over Jerusalem,

Jesus, moved with compassion for the widow of Naim,

Jesus, weeping with Martha and Mary,

Jesus, absolving and defending Magdalen,

Jesus, Who didst say to the woman taken in adultery,
  "Neither will I condemn thee; go and now sin no
  more,"[11]

Have mercy on us.

1	Psalm 129.	2	Hebrews 4.	3	John 1.
4	Hebrews 2.	5	Hebrews 2.	6	Prov. 17.
7	Prov. 18.	8	Jerem. 31.	9	Jonas 4.
10	Luke 15.	11	John 8.		

Jesus, sorrowful in the Garden,
Jesus, casting a look of mercy on Peter,
Jesus, promising Paradise to the penitent thief,
Jesus Christ, the same yesterday, today, and for ever,[1]

Have mercy on us.

Lamb of God, Who takest away the sins of the world,
   Spare us, O Lord.
Lamb of God, who takest away the sins of the world,
   Graciously hear us O Lord.
Lamb of God, who takest away the sins of the world,
   Have mercy on us.

V. We beseech thee therefore help Thy servants,
R. Whom Thou hast redeemed with Thy Precious Blood.

LET US PRAY:

O God, Who hast said, *I am He that blot out thy iniquities for My own sake, and I will not remember thy sins,*[2] blot out my iniquities, I beseech Thee, and remember my sins no more. Blot them out, for Thy own sake— to glorify Thy mercy and the Precious Blood of Thy well-beloved Son. Grant that I, to whom much has been forgiven, may love much. Stand by me in trial and temptation, and so strengthen me by Thy grace, that neither life nor death nor any creature may separate me from Thee. Amen.

---

1   Hebrews 13.   2   Isaias 43.

HOLY COMMUNION

HOLY COMMUNION

———

I am the Bread of Life. (John 6)
He that eateth Me, the same also shall live by Me.
(John 6)

———

EVERY conceivable motive urges us to make the most of our Lord's visits to us in Holy Communion—the dignity and the goodness of Him Who comes, the unworthiness and the need of those to whom He comes, the liberality with which He rewards all who prepare befittingly for His coming. "His Majesty is not wont to pay poorly for His lodging, if He be well received," says St. Teresa. And He Himself says, *I will glorify the place of my feet.*[1]

We feel our Lord deserves the best welcome we can give Him—a better welcome each time He comes. We desire to give it Him. Yet, in spite of our desires, rather

———

1   Isaias 60.

because of them, we feel the need of guarding against the deadening influence of routine by continually arousing our faith, that so the frequency of His visits and the familiarity He allows us, far from lessening our reverence and our love, may be ever increasing both.

Some find it helpful to consider in each Communion one of the relations in which our Lord stands to us, and to colour their preparation and thanksgiving with the thoughts which that relation suggests. One thought that has had time to sink into the mind and soak there is worth a hundred that have touched the surface and run off. Such a thought will bear fruit in the strong affections of the heart and in the firm resolves of the will, the result to which all preparation and thanksgiving should tend.

To those who follow this method in their preparation and thanksgiving, the following suggestions are offered, not as a set form to be adhered to, but as mere samples of what each of us may with profit do for ourselves. As in the *Preparation for Confession*, it is never supposed that the whole matter for one day will be used. A choice is offered to suit different tastes and moods.

St. Teresa says that these quarters of an hour after Holy Communion are the most precious of our lives, and theologians teach that, as long as the sacramental species remain within us, we receive, in virtue of the sacrament, grace proportioned to the fervour of the acts we make.

Surely, then, if there are in our lives *days of salvation* and *an acceptable time,*[1] they are our Communion days, with their time of thanksgiving. *Defraud not thyself of the good day* is the counsel of the Holy Spirit.[2] And our Lord Himself reminds us: *You have not Me always.*[3]

---

1   Isaias 49.   2   Ecclus. 14.   3   John 12.

I.

CHRIST OUR LORD AS THE SECOND PERSON OF THE BLESSED TRINITY

———

O Beata Trinitas!

———

(BEFORE COMMUNION)

I. WHO COMES?

The All-Holy, the Almighty, the Infinite God, Who, because He is Lord of all, makes Himself gracious to all.[1]

What hard thoughts of God were brought into the world by sin! *In the beginning,* the hearts of Adam and Eve bounded with joy *when they heard the Voice of the Lord God walking in Paradise at the afternoon air.*[2] They rejoiced exceedingly in the nearness of approach, in the familiar intercourse with Him Whom they loved.

Sin came and all was changed. Men began to think of the God Who made them as of a cruel tyrant, to

———
1   Wisdom 12.   2   Genesis 3.

be approached with terror and appeased with horrible sacrifices. Millions so think of Him now. There are millions in the world to-day who have these unworthy, these unfilial thoughts of God; who know dimly of an enmity long ago, and nothing of the healing, nothing of Him Who *is our Peace, Who has brought Heaven and earth together and made both one, breaking down the wall of partition, reconciling all things unto Himself,*[1] *through the Blood of His cross.*[2]

What shall be my thoughts who know all this so well, who know the lengths to which the reconciliation has gone, the depths to which the Creator has stooped to give us the kiss of peace; who know of a nearness of approach of which Adam and Eve never dreamed, of a morning Communion of which that walking with God in the afternoon air was but a beautiful foreshadowing!

O my God, my God, You Who care for the thoughts Your creatures have of You, give me such as are worthy of Your creature, so wonderfully created and more wonderfully restored—worthy of Your child. If I think hard thoughts of You now, after all You have done for me, do I not deserve to be among those *who shall be justly punished because they have not thought well of God.*[3] I will not do You this dishonour. Whatever I have to be punished for, it shall not be for

---

1 Ephes. 2.   2 Coloss. 1.   3 Wisdom 14.

this. *O Lord, Father and God of my life,*[1] *I will praise Thy name continually, and will praise it with thanksgiving.*[2] *My hope shall not be the hope of the unthankful.*[3] *Thou hast saved me from destruction, and hast delivered me from the evil time, therefore I will give thanks and praise Thee, and bless the name of the Lord,*[4] *and with all my strength I will love Him Who made me.*[5]

What must that goodness be out of which has come a Redemption such as ours! What a glorious array of infinite perfections must it enclose within itself! What must You be in Yourself, my God, that You can be so good to us! O highest Good, the only Good, *Who is like to Thee?*[6] Well may the Blessed be proud of their God! Well may they cry out, with their Prince and leader, "Who is like to God!" *Salvation to our God, Who sitteth upon the throne. Amen. Benediction and glory and wisdom and thanksgiving, honour and power and strength to our God for ever and ever. Amen.*[7]

---

1   Ecclus. 23.   2   Ecclus. 51.   3   Wisdom 16.

4   Ecclus. 51.   5   Ecclus. 7.   6   Psalm 34.

7   Apoc. 7.

Faith

My God! how wonderful Thou art,
  Thy Majesty how bright,
How beautiful Thy Mercy-Seat
  In depths of burning light!

How dread are Thine eternal years,
  O everlasting Lord!
By prostrate spirits day and night
  Incessantly adored!

How beautiful, how beautiful,
  The sight of Thee must be!
Thine endless wisdom, boundless power,
  And awful purity.

Oh, how I fear Thee, living God!
  With deepest, tenderest fears;
And worship Thee with trembling hope,
  And penitential tears.

Love

Yet I may love Thee too, O Lord!
    Almighty as Thou art;
For Thou hast stooped to ask of me
    The love of my poor heart.

Oh, then, this worse than worthless heart
    In pity deign to take;
And make it love Thee for Thyself
    And for Thy glory's sake.

II. To Whom Does He Come?

The great God, by Whom all things were made, comes to His little creature, poor, sinful, utterly unworthy of Him, innumerable times ungrateful to Him, but His creature still, and loved by Him with the blessed, persistent love of the Creator—*still*, in spite of all the past.

The Word made flesh for our redemption comes to one who has so often defrauded Him of the precious fruit of His Passion and Death, who has been such an unprofitable servant, such a faithless disciple, but whose sole desire now is to return Him love for love, to be all His, only His, His according to the desires of His Heart.

The Source of graces comes to one who has often grieved Him, often turned a deaf ear to His whisperings, to His invitations, to the desire for the better gifts, the more acceptable ways, the higher, fuller, more generous service of God, to which His promptings led.

Shall it be so always? Come, Lord, breathe where Thou wilt, lead where Thou wilt.

Humility

My soul! what hast thou done for God?
  Look o'er thy misspent years and see;
Sum up what thou hast done for God,
  And then what God hath done for thee.

He made thee when He might have made
  A soul that would have loved Him more;
He rescued thee from nothingness,
  And set thee on life's happy shore.

Had God in Heaven no work to do
  But miracles of love for thee?
No world to rule, no joy in self,
  And in His own infinity?

Oh, wonderful, oh, passing thought,
　　The love that God hath had for thee,
Spending on thee no less a sum
　　Than the Undivided Trinity!

What hast thou done for God, my soul?
　　Look o'er thy misspent years and see;
Cry from thy worse than nothingness,
　　Cry for His mercy upon thee.

Contrition

I have brought up children and exalted them: but they have despised Me.[1]

Thou hast forsaken the God that begot thee, and hast forgotten the Lord that created thee.[2] It is to me, my God, that these tender reproaches are made. I have forsaken You, O God, my Creator; I have forsaken You, O God, my Father. You have so exalted me as to make me Your child, only a little less than those elder *sons of God*, the angels. And I have forgotten and despised You, I have gathered together all Your gifts, and wandered away from Your face into a far country, and there wasted all. And You have not wearied of me. You have called me back to You. You have waited for me. You have come out to meet Your prodigal child,

1　Isaias 1.　　　2　Deut. 32.

and have taken me back to Your arms and to Your Heart. *Thou sparest all because they are Thine, O Lord, Who lovest souls.*[1]

O God of love, my Creator and my Father, I grieve from the bottom of my heart for all my sins. I grieve in particular for the sins of my childhood and my youth, the sins before I came into Religion. It is for them in particular I desire to make an act of loving and intense contrition. "I have sinned exceedingly in my life. What shall I do, whither shall I flee, *but to Thee, my God?*" Put into my heart the tender trustful sorrow of a prodigal child. I trust the past to Your mercy, and the future to Your providence. Keep me from all sin, never let me be separated from You, and then do with me what You will.

> I wish to have no wishes left
> But to leave all to Thee,

And yet

> One wish is hard to be unwished,
> That I at last might die
> Of grief for having wronged with sin
> Thy spotless Majesty.

---

1   Wisdom 11.

III. WHY DOES HE COME?

He comes to quicken joy and confidence in my heart by His embrace. He comes to support my tottering steps; to let me lean on His omnipotence; to make me feel in all my weakness that underneath are the everlasting arms.[1] He comes to help me towards the noble end for which He created me, *to make me worthy of the vocation in which* I am *called,*[2] a vocation not only to praise, revere, and serve Him, but to praise Him eminently, to revere Him eminently, as all are not called to do—to praise, revere, and serve Him perfectly. For this I need a strong grace. To bring it, the great God quits Heaven, and comes to me: *Veni Domine, noli tardare!*

He comes to renew in my soul the fruits of His redemption; to hear the renewal of my vows, my promises, my desires; to unite me intimately with Himself, that according to His promise I may live by Him, that He may be to me the pledge of life, that He may raise me up at the Last Day: *Veni Jesu, Domine!*

He comes to take possession anew of what was His from the beginning, to sanctify anew His sanctuary, and make it a holy of holies, the presence-chamber, the dwelling-place of God—consecrating anew to His

---

1   Deut. 33.   2   Ephes. 4.

service my body with all its senses, my soul with all its powers, uniting Himself now in a way so intimate that He alone can comprehend it, to prepare me thus for the union He designs for me in the life to come: *Veni Dator Munerum.*

Hope and Desire

All good things come to me with You, my God. You cannot help giving me all good in giving me Yourself. Wisdom and love, holiness, joy, peace, patience, sweetness—all these in their very essence will enter my soul as You cross the threshold. O God, the Supreme Good!

Tu es fortis; Tu es magnus; Tu es altissimus.

Tu es bonus, omne bonum, summum bonum, Domine Deus, unus et verus.

Tu es amor et charitas; Tu es humilitas; Tu es patientia; Tu es pulchritudo.

Tu es securitas; Tu es quies; Tu es gaudium; Tu es spes nostra, et lætitia; Tu es fortitudo, et prudentia.

Omnipotens, sanctissime, altissime, et summe Deus, summum bonum, omne bonum, totum bonum, qui solus es bonus, Tibi reddamus omnem laudem, omnem gloriam, omnem honorem, omnem benedictionem, et omnia bona Tibi referamus semper. Amen.

O little heart of mine! shall pain
Or sorrow make thee moan,
When all this God is all for Thee,
A Father all thine own?

(AFTER COMMUNION)

Adoration, Thanksgiving, Love

I fall down to adore You, O Holy and Undivided Trinity, One in Three and Three in One, the earliest, highest, dearest Mystery of our faith!

I fall before You and adore You, O Eternal Father, *Father of our Lord Jesus Christ, of Whom all paternity in Heaven and earth is named!*[1] Our Father, Who art in Heaven!   I love and praise You in union with the Son and the Holy Spirit, and together with my vow of poverty, put myself wholly into Your hand for ever.

Sume, Domine, et suscipe!

I fall before You, and adore You, O Eternal Son, God of God, Light of Light, very God of very God, my Brother by the Incarnation, my Spouse by the vows of my profession, my Redeemer, My Master, my All in all!

---

1   Ephes. 3.

I love and praise You in union with the Father and the Holy Spirit, and together with my vow of chastity, give myself wholly to Your Heart for ever.

Sume, Domine, et suscipe!

I fall before You and adore You, O Eternal Spirit, coequal with the Father and the Son, my Guide, my Comforter!

I love and praise You in union with the Father and the Son, Whose uncreated Love You are, and together with my vow of obedience, abandon myself wholly to Your leading, to be conformed in all things to Your will for ever.

Sume, Domine, et suscipe!

Adoration

Come, let us adore and fall down before the Lord that made us, for He is the Lord our God.[1]

Adoro Te devote, latens Deitas.

I adore You, O Lord, my Creator, O God my Redeemer, my Sanctifier, O Ever-Blessed and Undivided Trinity!

---

1   Psalm 94.

Holy, Holy, Holy, Lord God of hosts; the earth is full of Thy glory; Glory be to the Father; Glory be to the Son; Glory be to the Holy Ghost. (100 days.)

Glory be to the Father, Who created me out of love.

Glory be to the Son, Who redeemed me with love.

Glory be to the Holy Ghost, Who sanctified me in love, and reserved for me His graces of predilection.

Glory be to the Holy and Undivided Trinity, one God, for ever and ever. Amen.

Laudamus Te; benedicimus Te; adoramus Te, glorificamus Te. Gratias agimus Tibi propter magnam gloriam Tuam.

Thanksgiving

Te Deum laudamus: Te Dominum confitemur.
Te æternum Patrem: omnis terra veneratur.
Patrem immensæ majestatis.
Venerandum Tuum verum, et unicum Filium.
Sanctum quoque Paraclitum Spiritum.
Benedicamus Patrem et Filium cum Sancto Spiritu.
Laudemus et superexaltemus eum in sæcula.
Benedicta sit Sancta Trinitas et indivisa unitas, una Deitas!

O ye angels of the Lord, bless the Lord, praise and exalt Him above all for ever.

O ye sons of men, bless the Lord; praise and exalt Him above all for ever.

O ye servants of the Lord, bless the Lord; praise and exalt Him above all for ever.

O ye spirits and souls of the just, bless the Lord; praise and exalt Him above all for ever.

O ye holy and humble of heart, bless the Lord; praise and exalt Him above all for ever.

O give thanks to the Lord because He is good, because His mercy endureth for ever.

O all ye religious, bless the Lord; praise Him and give Him thanks because His mercy endureth for ever.[1]

Love

Is not He thy Father, that hath possessed thee, and made thee, and created thee?[2]

You are not your own, you are bought with a great price.[3]

You are the temple of God, and the Spirit of God dwelleth in you.[4]

To whom, my God, do I belong if not to You? Who else has a shadow of right to me? I am Yours by creation, by redemption, by sanctification. I am Yours

1   Daniel 3:58-90.   2   Deut. 22.
3   I Cor. 6.   4   I Cor. iii.

by the vows of my profession. And how have You treated one who is Yours by so many titles? Have You loved me? Have You given me cause to love You? Love is shown by deeds, by the communication of good things. Will Your love bear this test, my God? Oh, let the history of Your benefits to me throughout my life speak for You—that hidden history of Your dealings with my soul, the significancy of which I could not make known to others, even if I would—the opportunities, the help in need, the persistent drawing and waiting which make up the history of my life.

> No earthly father loves like Thee,
>   No mother half so mild
> Bears and forbears, as Thou hast done,
>   With me Thy sinful child.

I have cause indeed to love, and I tell You again and again that I love You, my God and my All. But where are the proofs? Love is shown by deeds. In deed and in truth You have loved me. But where are the proofs of my love? Resolutions in plenty every morning. But when the evening comes what have I actually done? Where has been the devotedness to Your interests, the dependence on You, the union with You, the alacrity in Your service, the love of You for Your own sake, the spirit of sacrifice which is the need and the food of love?

You have done much for me, my God, but there is still much that You can do. You can do for me what I cannot do for myself, You can free me from self, which usurps Your rightful place in my soul, and take what is Your own.

> With gentle swiftness lead me on,
>   Dear God! to see Thy face;
> And meanwhile in my narrow heart
>   Oh, make Thyself more space!

O ye Angels, Archangels, Thrones and Dominations, Principalities and Powers, Virtues of Heaven, Cherubim and Seraphim, adore our God for me; thank Him, and love Him with me. Patriarchs and Prophets, Apostles, all ye Martyrs of Christ, holy Confessors, Virgins of the Lord, and all ye Saints, adore Him, thank Him, love Him with me.

Mother of God, adore your Son for me, thank Him, and love Him for me.

O Heart of Jesus, be my adoration and my thanksgiving to the three Divine Persons now dwelling within me.

Eternal Father, look upon the face of Your Christ. Through Him and with Him and in Him be to You in the unity of the Holy Spirit all honour and glory. Amen.

Petition

What a joy it is, my God, to lay down my soul at Your feet, and feel that You read it through and through. I know what You see there. I know I ought to fear Your all-holy glance. And yet I love to think of You as my inward Witness. It is a joy to know that *Thou hast understood my thoughts*,[1] that there is nothing I can hide from You, even if I would. Bad as I am, I am content that you know all. I have no secrets from You, my God.

And so I lay my heart here at Your feet, and open it out before You. All its needs, all its miseries, all its longings are known to You—what it is, what it ought to be, what You want it to be. Take it into Your hands. Put it right for me. You can, and You have the will. You are its Maker; You know exactly what is wrong. What springs to touch You know, and what to cleanse, and what to renew.

> For Thou hast made this wondrous soul
>   All for Thyself alone;
> Ah! send Thy sweet transforming grace
>   To make it more Thine own.

Your interest and Your intentions are mine, my God, because they are Yours, I love and care for them

---

1   Psalm 138.

all, I pray for them every one. The interests of Your greater Glory; the accomplishment of Your Will; the extension of Your Kingdom—for all this I pray. For the Church suffering, the holy, waiting souls; for the Church militant, and her almost infinite needs; for the Holy See above all. I think of the weight of solicitude that day and night presses on the anxious head of the Vicar of Christ, his strength enfeebled, his resources cut off, the powers of the world leagued against him, and I pray for him. I pray for all rulers in Church and State; for all who can much advance or hinder the good of souls. I pray for all labourers in Your vineyard, for all who are now bearing the burden and heat of the day. And I beg for all Your pity, Your blessing, and Your help.

> Father, all we who toil on earth
>   One day at rest shall be,
> Thou art our haven and our home,
>   O dearest Trinity!

Oblation

My God, what can I give to You in return for all You have given to me? I give You my heart, I give You my love, I give You my body with all its senses, my soul with all its powers, my heart with all its affections.

I give You my vows. I give you all I have and am, now and always in time and eternity. I bring to You all I love, all my treasures, all who are dear to me, all who are in any way entrusted to me, and I give them all into Your keeping.

I trust to You my temptations, my graces, my responsibilities, my opportunities. I trust to You my progress in the way of perfection, my desire of a closer, more uninterrupted union with You. Bring me up to the ideal You had in Your Divine mind when You created my soul. I could not bear, my God, to fall short of Your designs after all You have done for me; I could not bear to be a disappointment to You throughout eternity.

> *Jesu, quem velatum nunc aspicio,*
> *Oro, fiat illud, quod tam sitio,*
> *Ut, Te revelata cernens facie,*
> *Visu sim beatus Tuæ gloriæ.*

O Jesu, Whom by faith I now descry,
    Shrouded from mortal eye,
When wilt Thou slake the thirsting of my heart
    To see Thee as Thou art,
Face unto face in all Thy glad array,
    Tranced with the glory of that everlasting day?

Prayer Before a Crucifix

EN EGO, o bone et dulcissime Iesu,
ante conspectum tuum genibus me provolvo,
ac maximo animi ardore te oro atque obtestor,
ut meum in cor vividos fidei, spei et caritatis sensus,
atque veram peccatorum meorum paenitentiam,
eaque emendandi firmissimam voluntatem velis
    imprimere;
dum magno animi affectu et dolore
tua quinque vulnera mecum ipse considero ac mente
    contemplor,
illud prae oculis habens,
quod iam in ore ponebat tuol David propheta de te, o
    bone Iesu:
"Foderunt manus meas et pedes meos:
dinumeraverunt omnia ossa mea." Amen.

BEHOLD, O kind and most sweet Jesus,
I fall upon my knees before Thee,
and with most fervent desire beg and beseech Thee
that Thou wouldst impress upon my heart
a lively sense of faith, hope and charity,
true repentance for my sins,
and a firm resolve to make amends.
while with deep affection and grief, I reflect upon Thy
    five wounds,
having before my eyes that which Thy prophet David
    spoke about Thee, o good Jesus:
"They have pierced my hands and feet,
they have counted all my bones." Amen.

II.

CHRIST OUR LORD AS JUDGE

———

Be at agreement with thy adversary betimes whilst
thou art in the way with him. (Matt. 5:5)

———

(BEFORE COMMUNION)

I. WHO COMES?

It is hard to think of You as an Adversary, dear
Lord. If You are not our Friend and our Advocate,
to whom shall we go? *If Thou, O Lord, shall observe*
iniquities, Lord, who shall endure it? Yet if adversary
means one who has much against us, we must own that
the hard name is just and take Your counsel home to
ourselves with trembling. But there is love, O Lord,
in Your every word to us. There is love in all Your
words, for they come every one of them from out

of Your Heart. And it is out of the depths of that Heart that Your most solemn words of warning come. We feel that love in Your warning here. Even as our Adversary, You take our part. You put Yourself in the way as we near the Judgment-seat, and urge us to a reconciliation while there is yet time.

Faith

I believe, my God, that You, Who in a very little while will be my Judge, are coming to me now in the most friendly of visits to teach me how I may come off safely at my trial, that trial on which my eternity depends.

Love

How can I thank You for goodness like this! I desire to receive You with exceeding love and gratitude. Help me to appease and gain You now by earnest prayer, that I may stand without fear before You in that dreadful day when there will be no more place for prayer.

> *Juste Judex ultionis*
> *Donum fac remissionis*
> *Ante diem rationis.*
>
> *Rex tremendæ majestatis,*
> *Qui salvandos salvas gratis,*
> *Salva me, fons pietatis.*

O just avenging Judge, I pray,
In pity take my sins away,
Before the great accounting day.

Thou King of dreadful majesty,
Granting Thy grace and mercy free,
Fountain of love, O save Thou me.

II. To Whom Does He Come?

To me, who have so much reason to fear His coming, who have been such an unprofitable servant, such a faithless steward.

Holy Job could say: *If I shall be judged, I know that I shall be found just.*[1] How different is the witness I must bear against myself: *That I have sinned exceedingly in thought, word, and deed, through my fault, through my fault, through my most grievous fault.* With David I must say: *Have mercy on me, O God, according to Thy great mercy*; and with the publican: *O God, be merciful to me a sinner.*

My God, how is it possible for pride to be one of the devil's temptations at the last? With Judgment so near, with the blinding light of Your holiness—the light from the great white throne—cast forward on the death-bed, how is pride possible? But if impossible then, how is it possible now? Judgment is near always;

---

1   Job 13.

the light from the throne is above us now and always; my life and every action of my life is being ever confronted with Your holiness; *now* the record is taken; *now* the judgments are given which the judgment after death will only confirm. Therefore the judgment now is in one sense of greater moment than the one I have so much reason to fear hereafter. And I can influence it. I can make it a Judgment of mercy—*then* it must be justice without mercy. Let my soul be always in the state in which I shall wish it to be when I have to meet You, my God. Let me be always ready for You, looking out for You, expecting You, preparing for You. Let me keep always in my heart Your word of warning—*Watch!*

Humility

He comes to me Who is the Judge of the living and the dead. Before Him the pillars of Heaven tremble, and the pure angels veil their faces with their wings. Whither shall I flee from His face? Two places are safe for me—the depths of my misery and the Heart of my Judge. In them will I hide myself.

Quid sum miser tunc dicturus?
Quem patronum rogaturus,
Cum vix justus sit securus?

What, guilty wretch, shall I then plead,
What patron ask to intercede,
When e'en the just assurance need?

Contrition

Cast me not away from Thy face on account of my
sins—the sins I have owned to You, my God, again
and again, the sins for which I have made so many
acts of contrition, the sins since I entered Religion, for
which I make a special act of contrition now. On Your
first word to me the moment after death my eternity
depends. O my Judge and my Saviour, it must, it
must be: *Come!* You will not find it in Your Heart to
cast me from You. You will find me some corner in
the place of purification where I may be prepared for
Your Presence. The Divine patience that has waited
for me so long will wait for me still, till the cleansing
fires have done their work. Then, *to the work of Thy
hands Thou shalt reach out Thy right hand,*[1] and say to
me again: *Come!*

---

1   Job 14.

Ingemisco tanquam reus,
Culpa rubet vultus meus:
Supplicanti parce, Deus.

Qui Mariam absolvisti,
Et latronem exaudisti,
Mihi quoque spem dedisti.

I groan beneath the guilt which Thou
Canst read upon my blushing brow,
But spare, O God, Thy suppliant now.

Thou Who didst Mary's sins unbind,
And mercy for the robber find,
Dost fill with hope my anxious mind.

III. WHY DOES HE COME?

Be at agreement with thy adversary betimes whilst thou
art in the way with him. It is for this He comes—to give
me the grandest of chances, the chance of going over
my accounts with Him whilst He is in the way with
me, whilst He is beneath my roof, my Guest, under
obligations to me, whilst He is a prisoner in my heart.
Could I have a more favourable opportunity? When
will my acts of contrition be made better than when
He is with me, prompting them, helping them? Once
forgiven now, no offence will be brought against me

later, and so He comes to me almost daily to forgive daily faults, that there may be no arrears left for the Judgment. If I make good use of His visits of mercy, shall I not be able to bear the searching scrutiny when the time of mercy is past—to stand without fear before my Judge Whom I have made my Friend when we were together in the way?

Hope and Desire

Surely, my God, if any one has cause to trust You it is I! Others may have their innocence or their virtues to fall back upon, but I have Your mercy, Your *great mercy*, only. I have made myself undeserving of it, but when have You ever treated me as I deserved? Where should I be now if justice and not mercy had had its way? O yes, *I trust You,* my God, *I trust You.* And if I could choose my Judge, I would choose You and no other. I know that *it is a fearful thing to fall into the hands of the Living God.*[1] Yet it is there I desire to fall when I come to die. My soul is my only one: I could not trust it except into the hands of Him Who made it. *Thy hands have made me and fashioned me.*[2] *Into Thy hands I commend my spirit.*[3]

---

1 Hebrews 10. 2 Job 10. 3 Psalm 30.

Recordare, Jesu pie,
Quod sum causa Tuae viæ:
Ne me perdas illa die.

Quærens me, sedisti lassus;
Redemisti, crucem passus:
Tantus labor non sit cassus.

Sweet Jesus think—my debt to pay
Thou wouldest tread the mournful way,
Forsake me not in that dread day.

In quest of me Thy feet were worn,
To ransom me Thy cross was borne,
Let not such love reap only scorn.

(AFTER COMMUNION)

Adoration

I adore You, O Judge of the living and the dead, before Whom I shall stand trembling in the hour of my death.

I adore You, my Judge, coming to me now in this visit of mercy. Have mercy on me and save me.

I adore You, O compassionate Adversary, ready to be at agreement with me now whilst we are together in the way.

I adore You, O my Judge and my Advocate, and lay my cause before You, and bless You beforehand for the sentence of mercy You will one day pronounce on me.

Thanksgiving

Blessed be Jesus Christ, true God and true Man.
Blessed be the Name of Jesus.
Blessed be His Most Sacred Heart.
Blessed be Jesus Christ in the Most Holy Sacrament
  of the Altar.
O Sacrament Most Holy, O Sacrament Divine,
All praise and all thanksgiving be every moment Thine.

Praise the Lord, O my soul, in my life I will praise the Lord, I will sing to my God as long as I shall be.[1]
Praise ye Him, all His angels: praise ye Him all His hosts.[2]
The Lord is great and exceedingly to be praised.[3]
O my soul, bless the Lord.[4]
Give glory to the Lord, for He is good: for His mercy endureth for ever.[5]

---

1   Psalm 145.   2   Psalm 148.   3   Psalm 95.
4   Psalm 103.   5   Psalm 106.

Love

Dear Lord, I come to You every now and then with my Communion of reparation. Oh, that I could come like Magdalen and soothe Your Heart as she did! What must have been the rain of those tears which You said *washed Your feet;* the number of those kisses which *never ceased!* O happy Magdalen! O sweet Communion of reparation! O blessed union of contrition and love!

Lord, may I hope to comfort You like this?

O ye Angels... (page 63).

Petition

Be at agreement with thy adversary whilst thou art in the way with him. It is for this that He comes—to put Himself at my disposal—to leave my sentence in my hands. O surely, Lord Jesus, I may dare to stand before You at death as my Judge, when You have prepared me Yourself during life, when You have Yourself heard my cause over and over again, and pleaded for me, and drawn from my heart contrition for all my sins, and united Your sorrow with mine. Only let me make use of Your visits of mercy in this *acceptable time* in these *days of salvation*—my Communion days. My God, cannot we come to an agreement! You desire my love with an infinite desire, I desire nothing so much as to love You. Give me Your love and Your grace, and this is enough for me. Surely, surely, my God, we are at agreement now.

Have pity, Lord, on the multitudes who never think of You as Judge, on those outside the Church who have but a dim belief in the judgment to come, and on those children of the Church who, believing firmly that it is coming and coming fast, think of it and prepare for it no more than if they did not believe. Remember, O Lord, that You *will have all men to be saved,*[1] and that You died for all, and since *the whole earth is made desolate because there is none that considereth in his heart,*[2] stir up faith in the hearts of all men. Give to all a living and practical faith in the judgment to come, that they may prepare for it while there is yet time.

Oblation (page 65).

---

1   1 Timothy 2.   2   Jerem. 12.

III.

CHRIST OUR LORD AS SAVIOUR

———

Behold thy Saviour cometh.—(Isaias 57)

———

I. Who Comes?

Awful must be the ruin that is the penalty of unforgiven sin, when God Himself calls it "*destruction;*" when He calls the highest bliss we can attain hereafter "*salvation*"—escape from that second death which is eternal; when He gives us His Incarnate Son by the name of "*Saviour!*" Our Lord is everything to us. He is the Head of our race. He is King, Master, Judge; the First-born among many brethren, our Friend and our Companion; the Way, the Truth, and the Life. He is our Food, our Treasure, our Last End. But before all and above all He is *Saviour*. Saviour is the

Name at which every knee bows in Heaven, on earth, and under the earth: *Thou shalt call His name Jesus, for He shall save His people from their sins.*[1]

Faith

I believe in God, the Father Almighty, Maker of Heaven and earth. . . . And in one Lord, Jesus Christ, the only-begotten Son of God, born of the Father before all ages, Who for us men, and *for our salvation*, came down from Heaven and was made man.

Love

O Deus, ego amo Te
Nec amo Te, ut salves me,
Aut quia non amantes Te
Æterno punis igne.
Tu, Tu, mi Jesu, totum me
Amplexus es in cruce,
Tulisti clavos, lanceam,
Multamque ignominiam,
Innumeros dolores,
Sudores et angores,
Ac mortem: et hæc propter me,
Ac pro me peccatore.
Cur igitur non amem Te
O Jesu amantissime?
Non ut in cœlo salves me,
Aut ne in æternum damnes me,

---

1   Matt. 1.

Aut præmii ullius spe;
Sed, sicut Tu amasti me,
Sic amo et amabo Te:
Solum quia Rex meus es,
Et solum quia Deus es.

My God, I love Thee, not because
I hope for Heav'n thereby;
Nor because they who love Thee not,
Must burn eternally.
Thou, O my Jesus, Thou didst me
Upon the cross embrace,
For me didst bear the nails and spear,
And manifold disgrace,
And griefs and torments numberless,
And sweat of agony,
E'en death itself—and all for one
Who was Thy enemy.
Then why, O Blessed Jesus Christ,
Should I not love Thee well;
Not for the sake of winning Heaven,
Nor of escaping hell;
Not with the hope of gaining aught,
Not seeking a reward,
But as Thyself hast loved me,
O ever-loving Lord?
E'en so I love Thee, and will love,
And in Thy praise will sing,
Solely because Thou art my God,
And my eternal King.

II. To Whom Does He Come?

To a fallen and an outcast race—fallen from their high dignity of children of God, outcast "in this vale of misery, as it were in exile among the brute beasts." He comes to sinners, to those who have added actual to original sin. *Christ hath loved us, and hath delivered Himself for us,*[1] *making peace through the Blood of His cross,*[2] *blotting out the handwriting of the decree that was against us, fastening it to the cross.*[3] He comes to all sinners: *Christ died for all.*[4] He gave *Himself a Redemption for all.*[5] He comes therefore to me: *He loved me and delivered Himself for me.*[6] *Christ Jesus came into the world to save sinners, of whom I am the chief.*[7] *No brother can redeem, nor shall man redeem: he shall not give to God his ransom nor the price of the redemption of his soul.*[8] But a Redeemer was found for us: *For God so loved the world as to give His only-begotten Son; that whosoever believeth in Him may not perish, but may have life everlasting.*[9]

Humility

Jesus, Jesus, be to me Jesus, and save me. Remember how You said: *The Son of man is come to seek and to save that which was lost.*[10] *They that are in health need not a*

1	Ephes. 5.	2	Coloss. 1.	3	Coloss. 2.
4	2 Cor. 5.	5	I Timothy 2.	6	Galat. 2.
7	I Timothy 1.	8	Psalm 48.	9	John 3.
10	Luke 19.				

physician, but they that are sick. I am not come to call the just, but sinners.[1] Dear Lord, I am sick, I am sinful, as You know, come to me and say: *I am thy salvation.*[2]

Contrition

He hath *borne the sins of many and hath prayed for the transgressors.*[3] He has borne my sins and He has prayed for me. O God, my Saviour, I grieve for all the sins of my life past, for those especially which have harmed the souls You love, by bad example, by negligence, by indifference. I grieve for whatever spiritual hurt or loss others have suffered through my fault. Make amends to them, I beseech You, from the inexhaustible treasures of Your Heart.

> *Pie Pelicane, Jesu Domine,*
> *Me immundum munda Tuo sanguine,*
> *Cujus una stilla salvum facere*
> *Totum mundum quit ab omni scelere.*

For me, dear Pelican, Thy bosom bled,
  For me Thy blood was shed.
Stained and polluted though my life has been,
  That blood can make me clean.
That blood whereof one precious drop could win
  Abundant pardon for a thousand worlds of sin.

---

1   Matt. 9.   2   Psalm 34.   3   Isaias 53.

III. Why Does He Come?

To be saved is all we ask for or desire. Our enemies have to be overcome, Heaven has to be reached, the possession of God to be secured, but we call it all *salvation*. Our Lord comes to *save us*. He has many sweet relations with us. He has many dear names. But Jesus, *Saviour*, comprises all. It is His name by predilection, the name He chose among all names. He would have it brought from Heaven at His Incarnation, He would have it fastened with Him to His cross. He loves to think of us as His Redeemed—bought with a great price, rescued and saved. And He loves to come to us bringing His salvation with Him. As He would trust the work of saving us to no other, so no other shall bring us this supreme gift. He must have the joy of bestowing it with His own hand. He is Himself the gift He brings, and as He crosses our threshold He says: *I am thy salvation;*[1] *this day is salvation come to this house.*[2] O what a Saviour we have in Jesus!

Hope and Desire

Well might Abraham rejoice to see His day, and Habacuc cry out in the fulness of his heart: *I will rejoice in God, my Jesus.*[3] Well might Zachary bless God for this *salvation from our enemies and from the hand of all that hate us,* and Mary say: *My spirit hath rejoiced in God, my*

---

1   Psalm 34.   2   Luke 19.   3   Hab. 3.

Saviour.[1] The glad message of angels at His birth was: *This day is born to you a Saviour.*[2] And the eternal alleluia of the saints will echo the same strain: *Salvation to our God Who sitteth upon the throne, and to the Lamb. . . . Alleluia. Salvation and glory and power to our God. Alleluia.*[3]

(AFTER COMMUNION)

Adoration

I adore You, O Soul of Christ, Holy of Holies, Holy with the holiness of God. I adore You, and annihilate myself before You in my emptiness, my nothingness, my baseness. Soul of Christ, sanctify me.

I adore You, Body of Christ—my Ransom on the cross, my Food in the Eucharist. O Divine Head, O Sacred Face, O compassionate Eyes, O blessed Hands and Feet, O loving Heart, I adore You, I love and praise You, I put my trust in You—Body of Christ, save me!

I adore You, most Precious Blood—life and healing, redemption, intercession—all in all to me. O Blood of my Saviour, by Your profuse generosity—under the olive trees, at the column of the scourging, on the altar of the cross—take away my languor and my apathy, take me out of myself, fire me with Your generosity, let me return You love for love—Blood of Christ, inebriate me!

---

1   Luke 1.   2   Luke 2.   3   Apoc. 7, 19.

Thanksgiving

Come, let us praise the Lord with joy, let us joyfully sing to God, our Saviour.[1]

Who hath loved us and washed us from our sins in His own Blood.[2]

My soul doth magnify the Lord, and my spirit hath rejoiced in God, my Saviour.[3]

Salvation to our God, Who sitteth upon the throne. . . . Alleluia. Salvation and glory and power to our God. Alleluia.[4]

Give glory to the Lord for He is good: for His mercy endureth for ever.[5]

For He is our peace,[6] *making peace through the Blood of His cross.*[7]

Blessed be God.
Blessed be His holy name.
Blessed be Jesus Christ, true God and true man.
Blessed be Jesus in the most holy Sacrament of
the altar.

Thanks be to God for His unspeakable gift.[8]

1	Psalm 94.	2	Apoc. 1.	3	Luke 1.
4	Apoc. 7, 19.	5	Psalm 106.	6	Ephes. 2.
7	Coloss. 1.	8	2 Cor. 9.			

Love

Lo, this is our God; we have waited for Him, and He will save us. This is the Lord; we have patiently waited for Him; we shall rejoice and be joyful in His salvation.[1]

My God and my Saviour![2]

Say to my soul: I am thy salvation.[3] *This day is salvation come to this house.*[4]

Behold, God is my Saviour: I will deal confidently.[5]

The Lord is my rock, and my strength, and my Saviour.[6]

He loved me and delivered Himself for me.[7]

Recordare, Jesu pie,
Quod sum causa Tuæ viæ,
Ne me perdas illa die.

Quærens me, sedisti lassus,
Redemisti, crucem passus,
Tantus labor non sit cassus.

O bone Jesu, exaudi me,
Intra Tua vulnera absconde me,
Ne permittas me separari a Te.

---

1   Isaias 25.   2   Psalm 61.   3   Psalm 34.

4   Luke 19.   5   Isaias 12.   6   2 Kings 22.

7   Galat. 2.

Sweet Jesus, think—my debt to pay,
Thou wouldest tread the mournful way;
Forsake me not in that dread day.

In quest of me Thy feet were worn,
To ransom me Thy cross was borne;
Let not such love reap only scorn.

O good Jesus, hear me;
Within Thy wounds hide me;
Never let me be separated from Thee.

O ye Angels... (page 63).

Petition

I thirst.[1] *Give Me to drink.*[2]

You thirst, O Lord, for my sanctification. Sanctify me Yourself by the close union that subsists between Yourself and me.

I thirst.[3] *Give Me to drink.*[4]

Lord, what shall I bring to Your thirsting Heart! Would that I could have lifted up to Your cross every soul for which You died, and have quenched Your burning thirst with its love and its contrition! Would that I could bring here to Your tabernacle the souls of all poor sinners—those who are near and dear to

1   John 19.   2   John 4.   3   John 19.
4   John 4.

me; those who have none to pray for them; those who are hardened in sin; who are bound by habits of sin; those who are to die today. Remember, O Saviour of all, that You died for all, and offered Yourself a Redemption for all, and *will have all to be saved.* "We beseech Thee, therefore, help Thy servants, whom Thou hast redeemed with Thy precious Blood."

Oblation (page 65).

IV.

CHRIST OUR LORD AS GUEST

———

Behold I stand at the gate and knock. If any man shall hear My voice and open to Me the door, I will come in to him and will sup with him, and he with Me. —(Apoc. 3.)

Come in, Thou Blessed of the Lord; why standest Thou without? I have prepared the house. —(Genesis 24.)

———

(BEFORE COMMUNION)

I. WHO COMES?

To think that Jesus Christ, *the Word of God,*[1] *the Only-Begotten Son, Who is in the Bosom of the Father,*[2] is coming to dwell with me! To think that Jesus of Nazareth, the Guest of Simon the Pharisee, the Guest of Zacheus, the dear Guest at Bethany, is to be my

———

1 Apoc. 19.   2 John 1.

Guest! The Son of the Living God, as Martha called Him, the Son of Man, as He loved to call Himself—coming *to me!* To think, nay, to know this with the perfect certainty of faith! Oh, why does not the expectation of such a visit move me more!

His Mother waited for Him in vain on the skirts of the crowd; the disciples at Emmaus had to press Him to go in and stay with them. And without any waiting or pressing He is coming *to me.*

Those who saw Him going into the house of Zacheus *murmured saying that He was gone to be a guest with a man that was a sinner.*[1] What must be the wonder of the saints and angels when they see Him come to my house—to be my guest, and coming from the highest Heaven, from the right hand of the Father! It was in the days of His lowliness on earth that *the Lord Jesus came in and went out amongst us*, as St. Peter says. But it is in the days of His glorious life that He comes to me.

When St. John saw in His glory Him on Whose breast he had leant at supper, he *fell at His feet as dead.*[2] How then can I draw near to Him without fear? Only because He is still *meek and humble of heart;*[3] Jesus Christ,

---

1   Luke 19.   2   Apoc. 1.   3   Matt. 11.

the same yesterday, today, and for ever;[1] and because upon me too He lays *His right hand, saying: Fear not.*[2]

Faith

My God, I believe with firmest faith that You Whom I am going to receive are the only-begotten Son of God, born of the Father before all ages, God of God, Light of Light, very God of very God, consubstantial with the Father by Whom all things were made. Who for us men and for our salvation came down from Heaven, and were incarnate by the Holy Ghost of the Virgin Mary, and were made man—Lord, increase my faith!

Love

I love You, O God made man for me! I desire to love You with all my heart and soul and mind and strength. I desire that every beating of my heart, every thought of my mind, every operation of my soul may be an act of love. I wish—oh, how I wish—that I could love You more!

---

1   Hebrews 13.   2   Apoc. 1.

II. To Whom Does He Come?

To me, who can do so little by way of preparation for His visit. Could I not do more, at least by doing more fervently what I do? He welcomes any preparation that is the outcome of love—welcomes it with all its shortcomings and imperfections. And He likes the various forms in which love manifests itself. The sisters of Bethany were very different characters; each had her own way of preparing for His visit. Martha was active and zealous. She thought more of the honour due to Him than of the pleasure to herself in His blessed company. The house must be at its best, all it had of value brought out, His friends invited, to make Him feel quite at home. All she could provide would never be good enough, so she went round and round up to the last moment, touching up here and there, seeing to all herself. Her mind was fixed on her Divine Guest as she went about her work, making all look bright and attractive for Him, Whom she believed to be the *Christ, the Son of the living God.*[1] And Mary's mind, too, was fixed on Him as she sat watching the road with those loving eyes and that eager heart of hers.

---

1   John 11.

Hope and Desire

O Lord and Master, You are my Guest as well as theirs. I wait and watch with them. Make me zealous, eager, longing, like Martha and Mary. Working and praying, I am preparing Your welcome. Let my heart be with You, let my work be for You always, always.

III. WHY DOES HE COME?

He that sat on the throne said: Behold, I make all things new.[1] O Emmanuel, God with us, truly, as our Guest in Holy Communion, You make all things new. Here it is the Guest Who provides the banquet, entertains His entertainers, *and passing, ministers unto them.* It is as our Guest in the Eucharist that You show us *it is more blessed to give than to receive.*[2] For You come to us with Your hands full of gifts seeking whom You may enrich.

Solomon gave the Queen of Saba all that she desired and asked of him, besides what he offered her of himself of his royal bounty.[3] But what was Solomon's bounty compared to Yours, my God! You come to give me more than I dare ask or desire. You come to purify me more and more; to strengthen in me the spirit of my vocation; to help me in all my work for You. You come to sanctify my body as well as my soul, that so it

---

1   Apoc. xxi.   2   Acts xx.   3   3 Kings x.

may deserve to rise one day in glory. You, Who are the Author of grace and the Giver of glory, come to lead me from grace to glory—to give me grace, which is the seed of glory.

Humility

Whence is this to me that my Lord should come to me? Who am I that all these treasures should be poured out upon me—that my Lord Himself should bring them to me and give them with His own hand! Lord, who am I that You should be mindful of me like this! Make me less unworthy of all You give me and do for me, less unworthy of the gift, which is Yourself.

Contrition

I come to You, my God, for contrition for my sins, for all my sins. Give me true sorrow for them all, in particular for all negligences You have seen in the observance of my vows, and for the little effort I have made to act in the spirit of my vows. I renew them here at Your feet in the spirit of loving contrition, humbly begging of Your infinite goodness and mercy that You will vouchsafe to admit this holocaust in an odour of sweetness, and that as You have already given me grace to desire and offer it, so You will also bestow plentiful grace on me to fulfil it. Amen.

(AFTER COMMUNION)

Adoration

Adoro Te devote, latens Deitas,
Quæ sub his figuris vere latitas;
Tibi se cor meum totum subjicit,
Quia Te contemplans totum deficit.

O Hidden God, devoutly unto Thee
    Bends my adoring knee;
With lowly semblances from sight concealed,
    To faith alone revealed.
Fain would my heart transpierce the mystery,
But fails and faints away, and yields itself to Thee.

Laudamus Te; benedicimus Te; adoramus Te;
glorificamus Te; . . . Domine Fili unigenite, Jesu Christe.
Tu Rex Gloriæ, Christe.
Tu Patris sempiternus es Filius.

We praise Thee; we bless Thee; we adore
Thee; we glorify Thee; . . . O Lord Jesus Christ,
the only-begotten Son.
Thou art the King of Glory, O Christ.
Thou art the Everlasting Son of the Father.

Ave verum Corpus, natum
  Ex Maria Virgine,
Vere passum, immolatum
In cruce pro homine.
O clemens, O pie,
O dulcis Jesu, Fili Mariæ.

Hail to Thee, true Body! sprung
  From the Virgin Mary's womb;
The same that on the cross was hung,
  And bore for man the bitter doom.
O kind, O loving One!
O sweet Jesus, Mary's Son.

My God, I adore You profoundly—as well at least as the darkness of this life and the feebleness of my faith will let me. When I make my first act of adoration in Heaven, I shall know for the first time what adoration is. To supply now for what is wanting to me, I offer You the profound adoration of Your angels and saints, as, prostrate around me, they pay their court to You. They adore and praise and thank You for me. I unite myself with them, I join them as well as I can; some day I shall be doing it all perfectly. Wait a little while, my God, wait till I find myself at the foot of Your throne, with every power of my soul set free—then, then I will adore You *in spirit and in truth.*[1]　*Have patience with me and I will pay Thee all!*[2]

Thanksgiving

Bless the Lord, O my soul, and let all that is within me bless His holy name.[3]

Bless the Lord, O my soul, and never forget all He hath done for thee.[4]

What shall I render to the Lord, for all that He hath rendered to me?[5]

I will pay my vows to the Lord in the courts of the house of the Lord, in the midst of thee, O Jerusalem![6]

Bless the Lord, all ye His angels, you that are mighty in strength.[7]

Give glory to the Lord, for He is good: for His mercy endureth for ever.[8]

For He hath satisfied the empty soul, and hath filled the hungry soul with good things.[9]

Blessed be the Lord for evermore. So be it, so be it.[10]

1　John 4.　　2　Matt. 18.　　3　Psalm 102.

4　Psalm 102.　　5　Psalm 115.　　6　Psalm 115.

7　Psalm 102.　　8　Psalm 106.　　9　Psalm 106.

10　Psalm 88.

Love

Whatever else is wanting in my welcome, O Lord, love must never be wanting. As You leave me, You must never turn round with that sad reproach: *Thou gavest Me no kiss.*[1] Your Heart is the most sensitive of hearts, keenly alive to kindness and unkindness. You notice, as we do, little marks of attention and affection from Your friends. You notice when they are wanting. Let my love be on the alert always. Let there be water for Your feet—the tears of true contrition. Let there be the fragrant perfumes of thanksgiving and praise. Above all, let there be the kiss of loving welcome. Never, never, Lord, say to me in sadness: *Thou gavest Me no kiss.*

O ye Angels... (page 63).

Petition

O Expectation of Israel, the Saviour thereof in time of trouble, why wilt Thou be as a stranger in the land, and as a wayfaring man turning in to lodge? Why wilt Thou be as a wandering man, as a mighty man that cannot save?[2]

---

1   Luke 7.   2   Jerem. 14.

When I think, O Lord, of the close intimacy between You and Your friends—those who shared their roof with You during Your life on earth, and, since then, the multitudes of holy ones whose hearts have been Your home—I feel how little I know You, though You have come to me as my Guest so many, many times. How long, O Lord, how long will You be as a stranger in the land? Why will You not make Yourself more to my soul? Why will You come and go, and let the remembrance of Your visits pass so quickly?

Stay with me, stay with me, O Lord. Keep up a loving communication between my heart and Yours after Your sacramental Presence has passed away. Let my heart be where my Treasure is. Let Your Divine Presence so absorb my mind, so fill my heart, that union with You may be the rule of my life, a union lasting on amidst the distractions of daily duties and cares, renewed rather than disturbed by contact with these things. Make them serve as reminders of You, and draw me *to* not *from* You, my God. The secret of my sanctification and of my efficiency as an instrument in Your hand lies in this union, in this inner life with You. Make it Your care to perfect it more and more. Make me content to leave God for God—to leave You in Your sacramental Presence to find You in Your creatures and in Your work. But let me long to be with You, when it is Your holy Will to permit it—and so there will come to be a sense of relief when I may put all aside to be with You.

Mane mecum, Domine—stay with me always, always, O Lord!

Why wilt Thou be as a stranger in the land? How lovely were Your tabernacles, O Lord, in this dear land, when its minsters were the shrines of Your real Presence! Now, like a wayfaring man, You turn in to lodge where You may.

You come unto Your own and Your own receive You not. Yet how many hearts would gladly lodge You, could they but find their way to You in the darkness! Give them, O Lord, the light for which they are crying. Give strength to all whom temporal motives keep out of the Church. And, since You are still lifted up daily all the land over, draw all hearts to Yourself.

Oblation (page 65).

V.

CHRIST OUR LORD AS MASTER

———

The Master is here and calleth for thee. —(John 11.)

———

(BEFORE COMMUNION)

I. Who Comes?

He of Whom it is written: *In the beginning was the Word, and the Word was with God, and the Word was God.*

All things were made by Him.[1] The human soul was made by Him and He understands thoroughly its nature and its needs. Its first need, its deepest need, is truth. The question of the Roman governor is the question of every soul that comes into this world: *What is truth?*[2] The Word of God, the eternal truth, alone can give the answer. And that He might give

---

1 John 1.   2 John 18.

it in the most persuasive of ways, through human lips, in human language, He took upon Himself our nature: *And the Word was made Flesh and dwelt amongst us.* And we saw Him, *the Only-Begotten of the Father,* in the synagogues and towns and villages, teaching humbly and patiently all who would learn of Him— our Divine Master, *full of grace and truth.*[1]

Ah, Lord, who shall say that *Master* is not one of the very dearest of Your names! Who can say that this name does not appeal to them, that it has no attractions for them? The Twelve would not say so, nor Martha, nor Magdalen. They would tell us it was the dear name by which You were known among Your own, the name ever on their lips: *You call Me Master and Lord;*[2] the name by which You willed to be known, which You Yourself put into their mouths: *Say, the Master saith.*[3]

Among the special kindnesses of God to Adam and Eve there is mention made of this—that He taught them: *Moreover, He gave them instructions.*[4] Flooded with light as they were, He satisfied more and more that hunger and thirst for truth which He Himself had given them. To us, who *see through a glass in a dark*

---

1   John 1.   2   John 13.   3   Matt. 25.

4   Ecclus. 17.

manner,[1] He has given the same craving. What is there highest and deepest in science, in poetry, in music, in art, that is not the soul's feeling after Him, the eternal truth, if *haply it may find Him?*[2] He Himself links the highest knowledge with life, and with life eternal: *This is eternal life to know Thee, the only true God and Jesus Christ Whom Thou hast sent.*[3]

This knowledge, the knowledge of You, my God, is the only knowledge I covet. I covet it with all my heart and soul and mind and strength, with a desire into which I throw all the vehemence of my soul.

Domine Jesu, noverim Te! Lord Jesus, let me know Thee, teach me to know Thee!

But the light I ask is not the cold, clear light of the arctic skies. It is a sunshine which shall warm and vivify and bring forth all the flowers and fruits of love.

Aspice me, ut diligam Te. Look upon me that I may love Thee. My God, Who art a *consuming fire,*[4] let there be nothing in me that can hide itself from Your heat—thoughts, words, deeds, intentions, affections, let all be purified thoroughly and penetrated through and through with the fire of Your love.

---

1   1 Cor. 13.   2   Acts 17.   3   John 17.

4   Hebrews 12.

Noverim me, noverim Te! Let me know myself, let me know Thee! By the low, dark entrance let me find my way into the brightness of Your Presence and come at length to Your feet.

> *Oderim me, et amem Te.*
> *Humiliem me, exaltem Te.*
> *Mortificem me, et vivam in Te.*
> *Fugiam me, confugiam ad Te.*
> *Voca me, ut videam Te.*
> *Et in æternum fruar Te.*

> Amen.

Let me hate myself and love Thee.
Let me humble myself and exalt Thee.
Die to myself and live in Thee.
Let me fly from myself and fly to Thee.
Bid me to come that I may see Thee.
And for ever and ever be happy in Thee.

Amen.

Faith

I believe with firmest faith that the Lord Who is coming to me is He Who taught the Twelve in the synagogues, in the corn-fields, on the mountain, on the lake, He for Whom the sisters at Bethany prepared and waited, Who gently chid the over-eager Martha, and kindled the heart of Mary as she sat listening at His feet. I believe that He is my Master no less than theirs, that He desires to speak to me, that He will speak to me, for—*For this am I come.*[1]

Love

Shall there not be in my heart something of Mary's eagerness when I hear those words: *The Master is come and calleth for thee?*[2] Shall I not rise up quickly and come to Him? Shall not my heart bound forward to meet Him with the cry, *Rabboni, Master!*[3]

O Lord and Master, chide me, if You will, I deserve it—chide me, not for overeagerness in my preparation for You, but for no preparation at all. I deserve Your reproaches and I will take them humbly and gratefully like Martha. But speak to me too as You spoke to Mary. Kindle my heart as You kindled hers: *Rabboni, Master!*

II. To Whom Does He Come?

Not to one of His quick learners—one of those who are a credit to Him. But to a dunce and an idler. Some there are who try even a Divine patience. I am one of these. I am backward, dull, forgetful, lazy, with

---

1 John 18.   2 John 11.   3 John 20.

little emulation, little courage and less perseverance. I have but the very feeblest grasp of truth. My mind has so little affinity with spiritual things that they are long in making any impression. I am slow in apprehending Divine principles and slower still in turning them into motives of action. And, worst of all, I am *slow of heart*. It is the heart that is at fault. My mind is furnished with principles that should make me a superb Religious. What is wanted is *practice*, that the light should pass from my mind to my heart and *rule my life*. I believe most firmly that I was created simply and solely to praise, revere, and serve God, and so to save my soul. And that all things I see around me are to be used or rejected in so far as they help or hinder me in the attainment of this my end. But has this fundamental truth mastered me as yet? Do I refer to it all that happens, everything around me—events, persons, weather, failure, success? Do I regulate my *choices* by it always? How different I should be if I did, if this one truth shaped my conduct, coloured my views, moulded my life! I know, my God, that You will never do great things by the soul that has but a feeble grasp of truth. I know too that You are content with the strong grasp of one truth, that this seized, all the rest follow. O Lord and Master, let this foundation truth take possession of my soul, let it work therein the change it has worked in so many. Then, from being weak, vacillating, unconcentrated, I shall become resolute, energetic, persevering—I shall be transformed.

Hope and Desire

Dear Master, do I not need You to speak to my heart? Speak then, for Your words are spirit and life. *O my God, be not Thou silent to me!*[1] *Let Thy voice sound in my ears.*[2] I do not deserve to hear You speak. I know that You are able *with one rough word to destroy.*[3] Yet again and again I entreat You to speak to me. Do not punish me by the master's keenest rebuke—silence. Do not let it be said of my Communions—*But Jesus was silent.*[4] You spoke to Pilate, for You pitied him and would have saved him. You spoke to the Canaanite who followed You with her pitiful cry, and bore meekly humiliation and delay, and looked up into Your face with perfect trust whilst You *answered her never a word.*[5] She knew with a woman's instinct that if she could but unseal those Divine lips, her cause was won. With her I cry out again and again: *Have mercy on me, O Lord, Thou Son of David.* With her I come

---

1   Psalm 27.   2   Cant. 2.   3   Wisdom 12.

4   Matt. 26.   5   Matt. 15.

and adore You, saying: *Lord, help me.* With her I wait
for the words: *Be it done to thee as thou wilt.*

III. WHY DOES HE COME?

He comes to teach me. *Good Master, what shall I do
to possess everlasting life?* [1]

Come to Me that you may have life. [2] *The words that I
have spoken to you are spirit and life.* [3]

He comes to teach me, to lead me into solitude
and there to speak to my heart. He is so one with
me in Holy Communion that I do not break in upon
His solitude nor He upon mine: *He was alone and His
disciples also were with Him.* [4] Teach me, dear Master, as
we are alone together. Only let me hear those words: *I
have somewhat to say to thee.* [5] And I will answer eagerly:
Master, say it. Speak to *my* heart. It is my heart that
wants teaching. I say it to my shame, for this ought
not to be. I am not one of those who live beneath
frigid skies, who never see the sun half their lives,
on whom none but his slant rays fall. I live and have
lived, oh, how many years in the full blaze of Your
Presence. How is it then that I contrive to hide myself
from Your heat? I take my beads and the mysteries of
Your blessed life pass before me—winning, wounding,

1	Luke 18.	2	John 5.	3	John 6.
4	Luke 9.	5	Luke 7.		

gladdening—yet they leave me scarcely moved. Each morning I am present on Calvary. Above me is the Church triumphant, intent upon the mystery to be accomplished there. Around and below is the Church militant and the Church suffering crying to me for help. But I am listless and distracted, and the half hour passes, and I go down the hill to my work with the Divine treasures put into my hands for distribution all but wasted, so far as depended upon me.

Dear Master, do I not need You to speak to my heart? Do not punish me by silence. But speak to my inmost heart—Your words are *spirit and life.*[1]

Humility

Who am I, to have the God-Man for my Master and Teacher? I think of those old heathen sages whose lives were spent in the search after truth. I hear their cry: *Which of us can go up to Heaven to bring it unto us, . . . which of us can cross the sea and bring it unto us?*[2] And I think what their thoughts would have been had they heard of the Incarnation—how for us men and for our salvation the Word of God *came down from Heaven and was made Man.* What their thoughts would have been had they heard of a closer union still: *The Word is very*

---

1   John 6.   2   Deut. 30.

nigh unto thee, in thy mouth and in thy heart.[1] *O Word
of God, Who came into the world . . . to give testimony to
the truth,*[2] Who come into our hearts to teach us all
truth, what would they have felt could they have sat at
Your feet and listened to Your words, could they have
received You but once into their heart!

Contrition

What must I feel who have made so little account
of Your blessed words—the words that I hear again
and again in the Gospel, that I hear times without
number in the secrecy of my own soul! How often
have I turned a deaf ear to Your reproaches, Your
inspirations, Your invitations! I hear what others
longed to hear and have not heard. And what I have
heard I have despised. That has been given to me
which would have transformed their lives, and I have
cast it away as worthless.

My God, I thank You from the bottom of my
heart for having placed my life *after*, not before, the
Incarnation, with the helps of holy Church and of
religion to sanctify it, rather than amidst the darkness
of infidelity or error. But what a careless life it has
been! I am sorry with all my heart for wasting what

---

1   Deut. 30.   2   John 18.

was Yours more than mine. I am sorry in particular for all my transgressions of Rule through sloth, cowardice, or human respect, for all the bad example I have thus given. *Abyss calleth upon abyss.*[1] I have sinned exceedingly in my life. Whither shall I fly *but to Thee, my God.* Thou wilt be propitious to my sin, *for it is great.*[2]

(AFTER COMMUNION)

Adoration

Rabboni! Master!—the cry of Faith.

> *Adoro Te devote, latens Deitas,*
> *Quæ sub his figuris vere latitas;*
> *Tibi se cor meum totum subjicit,*
> *Quia Te contemplans totum deficit.*

O Hidden God, devoutly unto Thee,
  Bends my adoring knee;
With lowly semblances from sight concealed,
  To faith alone revealed.
Fain would my heart transpierce the mystery,
But fails and faints away, and yields itself to Thee.

---

1   Psalm 41.   2   Psalm 24.

That He Who lay on Mary's knee,
Who still'd the waves of Galilee,
Was the dear Guest at Bethany,
And bled and died on Calvary,
That He in truth abides with me
I hold with faith's sure certainty.
O God, O hidden Deity,
Profoundly I here worship Thee,
Rabboni!

Thanksgiving

Rabboni! Master!—the cry of Praise.

Laudamus Te; benedicimus Te; adoramus Te; glorificamus Te. Domine Fili unigenite, Jesu Christe.

Tu solus sanctus, Tu solus Dominus; Tu solus altissimus, Jesu Christe, cum Sancto Spiritu in gloria Dei Patris.

Amen.

We praise Thee; we bless Thee; we adore Thee; we glorify Thee, O Lord Jesus Christ, the only-begotten Son.

Thou only art holy, Thou only art the Lord, Thou only, O Jesus Christ, with the Holy Ghost, art most high in the glory of God the Father.

Amen.

O God, most wonderful in all Thy ways,
Most in this mystery of Love, upraise
My heart to Thee in canticles of praise,
                    Rabboni!
And since my hungry soul this day is fed
With "meat indeed," with Thee the living Bread,
Give me to live by Thee as Thou hast said,
                    Rabboni!

Love

Rabboni! Master!—the cry of Welcome that should meet You, Lord, each time You come. It was Mary's act of faith, and adoration, and thanksgiving, and admiration, and joyful praise as she fell at Your feet in the garden of the Resurrection. You could trust that eager heart to seek until it found, and so You showed Yourself to her at first as the hidden God. Her eyes, her ears, her faith even, all but her heart was at fault till You called her by her name, *Mary! Rabboni!*

O Lord and Master, everything in me is at fault except my faith. Adoration and thanksgiving, and love, and admiration, and joyful praise—oh, where are these? But deep in my heart is the faith from which all these will spring at the sound of Your voice. Speak, Lord, call me by my name. Hide not Your face from me always. You may lift the veil a little and still remain the hidden God. Shall I not be blessed who have not seen like Mary, but have believed? *Lord, help Thou my unbelief!*[1] Let my faith be ever brightening till it brings me to the brightness of Your Presence and in a transport of love I fall before Your unveiled face, crying with greater joy than Mary's, *Rabboni! Master!*

O ye Angels... (page 63).

Petition

One is your Master, Christ.[2] In two ways, Lord, You are my Master. You are not Teacher only, You are Owner. I am not merely Your disciple, I am Your indisputable property. Thanks be to God that it is so. All that I have and am belongs to You—time, talents, labour, health, life, all the senses of my body, all the faculties of my soul. Take them, O Lord, they are Yours, to You I restore them. See that I do not misuse any one of them. See that I use them all with a pure intention for Your glory, for Your greater glory—choosing the means which *most* tend to the end for which I was created, by which I may love and follow You more closely.

---

1   Mark 9.   2   Matt. 23.

Have pity, O Lord and Master, on the poor, the suffering, the tempted, the uncared-for little ones. On the teeming races of the poor heathen all the world over. On the poor suffering souls in purgatory.

Oblation (page 65).

VI.

CHRIST OUR LORD AS FRIEND

———

Such is my Beloved and He is my Friend.—(Cant. 5.)

———

(BEFORE COMMUNION)

I. WHO COMES?

Love, for *God is love.*[1] I come back again to the dear familiar thought—the love and the loveableness of my God.

The Divine nature is love. It seeks to communicate Itself, to give of Its fulness: *Thou openest Thy hand and fittest with blessing every living creature.*[2] *Thou lovest all things that are, and hatest none of the things that Thou hast made: for Thou didst not make anything hating it. . . . O Lord, that lovest souls.*[3]

---

1   I John 4.   2   Psalm 144.   3   Wisdom 11.

Human history is a history of Divine love. *The mercy of the Lord is from eternity unto eternity.*[1] It seems hardly fair to You, my God, to call the Old Law the law of fear. The full revelation of Yourself in Your Gospel was reserved for the law of love, and so You were truly a hidden God amid the shadows of that olden time. But Your infinite sweetness was for ever, betraying You by all manner of winning words and ways, and tender reproaches, and immense compassions. Even then men were bid *to see that the Lord is sweet.*[2]

In His human nature too *God is love. The Image of the invisible God,*[3] *the Figure of His Substance,*[4] His Word, *was seen upon earth and conversed with men.*[5] *The Word was made Flesh and dwelt amongst us.*[6] And we saw Him in Whom *dwelleth all the fulness of the Godhead corporally,*[7] *full of grace and truth*, and tenderness, and pity. In every movement of eye, and lips, and hands, *the goodness and kindness of God our Saviour appeared.*[8] We were prepared for this. It was a delight rather than a surprise to recognize the Father *in the Son of His love.*[9] It was a delight to see how that perfect human Heart is perfect in Its human affections and in Its human

---

1	Psalm 102	2	Psalm 33.	3	Coloss. 1.
4	Hebrews 1.	5	Baruch 3.	6	John 1.
7	Coloss. 2.	8	Titus 3.	9	Coloss. 1.

friendships. Could it have been otherwise? Could the most perfect of hearts fail to prize the blessedness of friendship? Jesus prized it. He welcomed love and sympathy wherever they were to be found—in His Immaculate Mother, whose heart beat in perfect unison with His, in the poor sinner who loved much and was forgiven, in His rough-spoken, tenderhearted Apostles. He welcomed it in the voice from the crowd that lifted itself up in praise, in the wailing that followed Him to Calvary, in the dying thief's defence of Him from his cross. He is the same still. He has His friendships still. And all through the history of His Church we see the same predilections that showed themselves in the house at Bethany, and along the way of the cross. Not only to the hearts of the women of Jerusalem does His Heart appeal, but to the heart of Agnes, and Gertrude, and Teresa, and Margaret Mary. O tender Heart of Jesus, well might St. Paul cry out: *If any man love not the Lord Jesus Christ let him be anathema.*[1]

We are filled with wonder to hear the God of Heaven and earth call Abraham His friend: to hear Him say to His chosen Twelve: *I have not called you servants but friends.* But what shall we think when we

---

1   I Cor. 16.

see Him coming with His confidences, His sorrows, His desires, *to the weak things of this world*—coming to them again and again with the command: *Go tell My brethren*—coming to them, choosing them, because of their weakness, no doubt, but also—who can question it—because of their power of sympathy!

Faith

O Son of man, I delight to see all through the history of Your Church the tender human love of Your Sacred Heart. I thank You for offering Yourself to each of us in our journey through life as *our Friend*. It is a lonely journey, dear Lord, at times very lonely. Love and devotedness may surround us on every side, but there are depths and needs in the soul which only a Divine friendship can reach.

> Oh, I am glad to come to Thee,
>   My only rest,
> To lay my weary head awhile
>   Upon Thy breast,
> To bring the burden of my grief
>   Hither to Thee,
> And feel, O Jesus, Son of man,
>   Thy sympathy.

Love

Oh, that I could love You as if I had knelt at Your feet, and felt the touch of Your hand on my head, and heard the tones of the voice that uttered absolutions and gave vocations. As the poor and the sick of Galilee loved You, as the Apostles loved You, as she loved, who knew You best of all—*as You have loved me, Lord!*

At least let me love You with all my heart and soul and mind and strength. And let my love be worthy of the name—showing itself by confidence, by generosity, by sacrifice—acknowledging joyfully that all You do is right—counting no cost when I work for You—giving up cheerfully what is dear to me when You ask it, when it will help to Your better and fuller service.

My God, were any other in the place of Your Divine Majesty, it seems to me, He could not care in the very least for love such as mine—love so unworthy of the name, so unlike the love with which You have loved me—love so barren, so ungenerous, so unprepared for labour and sacrifice. How is it, O devoted and most faithful Friend, that You *can* care for love like mine? Only because You care *for me*, a greater mystery still.

How Thou canst think so well of us,
    Yet be the God Thou art
Is darkness to my intellect
    But sunshine to my heart.

II. To Whom Does He Come?

Not to Peter nor to John, not to Teresa nor to Margaret Mary, but to one who has nothing better to bring Him than desires. Happily He does not account them nothing. Nay, He sets great store by them. To Daniel, *the man of desires*,[1] was revealed the time of His coming, Who was *the Desired of all nations*.[2] To Simeon because of his desires was given the answer that he should not see death till he had seen the Christ of the Lord.

You, Lord Yourself, *desired with desire*. Desires are a language You understand perfectly, and the desires of the least among us. I am not to say: *I shall be hidden from God, and who shall remember me from on high? In such a multitude I shall not be known, for what is my soul in such an immense creation.*[3] *For He hath set His eye upon our hearts,*[4] *. . . and every heart is understood by Him.*[5] *The Lord hath heard the desire of the poor; Thy ears, O Lord,*

---

1   Daniel 10.   2   Aggeus 2.   3   Ecclus. 16.
4   Ecclus. 17.   5   Ecclus. 16.

have heard the preparation of the heart.[1] *Hear my prayer, O Lord, give ear to my tears.*[2]

My God, what account You make of the desires of the heart! How You must listen *to hear* our desires, *to hear* the preparation of the heart, *to hear* the falling tears. Listen to my desires, O Lord.

Hope and Desire

As the hart panteth after the water-brooks; so my soul panteth after Thee, O God.[3]

My soul hath thirsted after the strong living God.[4]

III. WHY DOES HE COME?

To bring home to me more and more that dear reality: *I also have a heart as well as you.*[5]

A father devises for his child a gift which it could never have entered into its mind to desire, or even to dream of. But once given, the gift seems the most natural and necessary thing in the world, and simply indispensable to the child's happiness. So is it with the Incarnation, that supreme Gift of God to man, the mighty, tender mystery which is entwined with every fibre of our daily life. No created intelligence could have suspected its possibility. If by impossibility the idea of it could have entered our

---

1   Psalm 9.   2   Psalm 38.   3   Psalm 41.

4   Psalm 41.   5   Job 12.

minds, should we have dared, my God, to ask for it, if not by prayer, at least by desire? Could I have dared to say to You: "O Lord, our Creator, You have commanded us to know You and to love You; but You are too far above us for this. If You would come within reach of us we would do it, for our minds leap up to You, and the hearts You have made for Yourself feel after You and yearn for You. Put Yourself within our reach, O Lord, our God. Oh, that You could but come amongst us as one of ourselves." *"Oh, that Thou wouldst rend the heavens and come down."*[1] What we all want, what I want, is to love and be loved by One Who has my human nature. I want Him to sit by my side and hold my hand and let me lean upon His breast. I want to tell my difficulties into a human ear. I want to confide my sorrows to a heart that feels like mine, that has suffered like mine, that can give me the help of its human sympathy, that has been weak with me, and has trembled before pain like me, that knows by its own experience all I have to tell it. My God, I think I could have looked up to You and longed for this and said it, if I dared—said to You trembling: "This is what it longs and asks for, the heart that You have made for Yourself. Does it ask too much?"

---

1   Isaias 64.

And You look down upon me and say: "Ah, child, how little You understand the love of the Creator. No, you have not asked too much; you have not asked enough. My knowledge of your needs is greater, My love is stronger than it has entered into your heart to conceive. And I am prepared to do for you more than you could ask or imagine. Not only to come within your reach, not only to live a human life before your eyes, not only to sit by your side and hold your hand and lay your head upon My Heart, but to come nearer still—to enter into your heart and there to hear all you have to tell Me—there to give you all you need—there to share with you My treasures.

No, you have not asked too much. But tell Me now, what use do you make of the gift of My real Presence in your midst—of the ever-ready sympathy of My human Heart? How often do you come to Me for help and strength and counsel? Ah, child, you have all and more than you could dare to ask, and still have I not to say sorrowfully: *Didst thou but know the gift of God!*[1]

---

1   John 4.

Contrition

You give to us, my God, with unstinted hand always. Your *gifts are without repentance.*[1] You repented that You made man, but You have never repented of the gift to us of Yourself. You saw all that was to come—the lonely tabernacles where no foot would cross the threshold, save once a week and then only from fear of sin. You saw the humiliations to which You would be exposed by accidents as well as by sacrilege. Yet the gift of Yourself You have never repented.

But I repent, O Lord—and oh, how much room for repentance there is. How bitterly I repent my neglect of You; my coldness towards You in the Sacrament of Your Love; the want of heart You have seen so often in my preparation for Communion and in my thanksgiving; my cruel neglect of You in Your prison on the altar. *Is this thy kindness to thy friend? Why wentest thou not with thy friend?*[2] my angel has said to me many a time, as I saw Him borne along in procession, or carried companionless and unhonoured to the sick. Could I not have spared a few moments and followed Him a little way? *Where thy treasure is, there is thy heart also.*[3]

---

1   Romans 11.   2   2 Kings 16.   3   Matt. 6.

Our Lord is in the tabernacle *for me*. He is there to be my Companion, *my* resource, *my* treasure, *my* Friend. Apart from every one else in the house, He would be there *for me*. He waits there *for me*. Has my behaviour towards Him during past years been any sort of a return for love like this? Do I make it worth His while to stay there, day after day, year after year *for me?*

O my Friend and my Treasure, let my heart draw me to You more and more in the lonely tabernacle, where You wait for me day and night.

Humility

Without Me, you can do nothing.[1] I know this, Lord, to my cost, or rather, I am grateful for the experience that has taught me this. I would rather have my strength in You than in myself. I would rather be a branch than a vine.

It is said of Abner, that he sent messengers to David, saying: *Make a league with me, and my hand shall be with thee. And he said: Very well, I will make a league with thee.*[2]

Make a league with me, O Lord. Be with me, my Friend, in all that I do, for *I can do all things in Him that strengtheneth me.*[3]

---

1   John 15.   2   2 Kings 3.   3   Philipp. 4.

(AFTER COMMUNION)

Adoration

Adoro Te supplex, latens Deitas.

Laudamus Te, benedicimus Te, adoramus Te, glorificamus Te.

Verily thou art a hidden God, the God of Israel, the Saviour.[1]

> O Jesus, hidden God, I cry to Thee,
> O Jesus, hidden Light, I turn to Thee,
> O Jesus, hidden Love, I run to Thee,
> With all the strength I have I worship Thee,
> With all the love I have I cling to Thee,
> With all my heart I long to be with Thee,
> And fear no more to fail or fall from Thee.

Thanksgiving

My soul doth magnify the Lord, and my spirit hath rejoiced in God, my Saviour, for He hath regarded the humility of His handmaid.[2]

Blessed be the Lord for evermore. So be it. So be it.[3]

Benedictus qui venit in nomine Domini. Hosanna in excelsis.

---

1   Isaias 45.   2   Luke 1.   3   Psalm 88.

Blessed be Jesus Christ true God and true man.

Blessed be the name of Jesus.

Blessed be His most Sacred Heart.

Blessed be Jesus in the most Holy Sacrament of the Altar.

Thanks be to God for His unspeakable gift.[1]

Love

And when they had adored God and given Him thanks they sat down together.[2] So is it with You, dear Lord, Friend *more friendly than a brother.*[3] You help me to adore and give thanks, and then You sit down to hear what I have to tell You. Sometimes to hear nothing, because I have nothing to say—my heart is hard and dry and wandering. Sometimes to hear nothing—not because I have nothing to say, but because there is no need to say it—the height of friendship is to be able to sit together, without conversation being obligatory.

You suit Yourself to me. You bear with me in my changing moods—bear with me when I can hardly bear with myself, my patient, compassionate, self-forgetting Friend.

---

1   2 Cor. 9.   2   Tobias 11.   3   Prov. 18.

Jesus, why dost Thou love me so?
    What hast Thou seen in me
To make my happiness so great,
    So dear a joy to Thee?

Wert Thou not God, I then might think
    Thou hadst no eye to read
The badness of this selfish heart,
    For which Thine own did bleed.

But Thou art God and knowest all;
    Dear Lord, Thou knowest me;
And yet Thy knowledge hinders not
    Thy love's sweet liberty.

Ah, how Thy grace hath wooed my soul
    With persevering wiles!
Now give me tears to weep; for tears
    Are deeper joys than smiles.

Each proof renewed of Thy great love
    Humbles me more and more,
And brings to light forgotten sins,
    And lays them at my door.

The more I love Thee, Lord! the more
    I hate my own cold heart;
The more Thou woundest me with love,
    The more I feel the smart.

What shall I do then, dearest Lord!
    Say, shall I fly from Thee,
And hide my poor unloving self
    Where Thou canst never see?

Or shall I pray that Thy dear love
    To me might not be given?
Ah, no! love must be pain on earth,
    If it be bliss in Heaven.

O ye Angels... (page 63).

Petition

I also have a heart as well as you.[1] *Yes, Lord, and of its fullness we have all received.*[2] It is close to my heart now; let virtue go out from It to mine. Make me like You in my dealings with others—gentle, indulgent, self-sacrificing, self-forgetting, self-sinking. No one ever sank self as You did. Give me Your helpful charity, Your sweetness, Your patience, Your long-suffering, Your power of sympathy. All these are in Your Heart, Lord, let them overflow into mine. You see how much I want them. Give me what I want. Help me. Make haste to help me. Remember that Your Holy Spirit says to us: *Say not to thy friend: Go and come again, and*

---

1 Job 12.   2 John 1.

to-morrow I will give to thee, when thou canst give at present.[1]
Give me to-day, give me now what I want, O Lord.
See how I knock and knock again at the door of Your
Heart. If You will not open to me because I am Your
friend, open because of my importunity.

I commend to You, dear Lord, all Your friends, all
Your faithful servants on earth, all on whom You have
great designs. So much depends on their reaching
their destined height. Think of Your glory which
is concerned, of the souls they have to help, and give
them in abundance all needful grace.

Oblation (page 65).

---

1   Prov. 3.

VII.

CHRIST OUR LORD AS KING

Behold your King.—(John 19)

(BEFORE COMMUNION)

I. Who Comes?

He, Who is King of kings, and Lord of lords,[1] *the King of glory,*[2] *a powerful King and greatly to be feared, Who sitteth upon His throne and is the God of dominion.*[3] He of Whom it is written: *On His head were many diadems.*[4] *Thousands of thousands ministered to Him, and ten thousand times a hundred thousand stood before Him.*[5] *And the armies that are in Heaven followed Him.*[6]

And the four-and-twenty ancients fell down before Him and adored Him—and cast their crowns before the throne.[7]

1	Apoc. 19.	2	Psalm 23.	3	Ecclus. 1.
4	Apoc. 19.	5	Daniel 7.	6	Apoc. 19.
7	Apoc. 4.				

Afterwards He was seen upon earth, and conversed with men.[1]

Art Thou a King then? . . . I am a King. For this was I born and for this came I into the world.[2] *I am appointed King over Sion.*[3]

Yet how little He parades His royalty. Among the things that are so sweet in the character of our King, is the absence of condescension about Him. He says so little about Himself. He comes so silently into our midst. He drops so quietly into our ways that we have to be continually reminding ourselves Who He is. Kings never succeed in putting those around them quite at their ease. They betray themselves unconsciously by the attentions they exact. "Do you forget," said one, "that I am your king." With the King of kings it is not so. He does not show us that He is stooping to come among us, that He feels our companionship trying, after what He has been used to, that our ways and our rudeness jar on His infinite refinement. No, He leaves St. Paul to speak about the annihilation of His Incarnation: *Taking the form of a servant, being made in the likeness of men, and in habit, found as a man.*[4] He Himself seems to be, if we might

---

1   Baruch 3.   2   John 18.   3   Psalm 2.

4   Philipp. 2.

venture to say so, proud of what He gained by His coming. He loves to call Himself the *Son of Man*. And once among us, He tries to be like us as far as He can. What we have to do and bear, He will do and bear, and as we take our daily privations and troubles as a matter of course, so will He. He speaks so seldom of Who He is, that some have said, He has never told us plainly that He is God. If He works miracles all day long during the three years of the public ministry, it is for our sakes, and He only speaks of them when our good requires that He should speak. Of His frightful sufferings He scarcely makes any mention— two or three times, that is all—and so calmly, quite as a thing to be looked for. When they were over, He said they were only what we ought to have expected our Messiah to do for us. *Ought not* Christ to have suffered these things? *These things,*[1] as if the mocking, and the scourging, and the crucifixion, which had completely staggered the faith of His disciples, were nothing so very wonderful after all.

Cur igitur non amem Te
O Jesu amantissime!

---

1   Luke 24.

O dearest King, who will give me a single reason in the wide world why I should not love You, why I should not dedicate to You every fibre of my being, why I should not strive with all my heart and soul and mind and strength to return You love for love?

Faith

It is a great glory to follow the Lord.[1]

I know it, O Lord, I know it. And I know how utterly unworthy I am to be ranked among Your followers, Your personal attendants, Your friends. I cannot understand in the very least how You can have chosen me. But I make my act of faith without understanding, and so come to Your feet, that by union with You I may become a little less unworthy.

Love

Thou also wast with Jesus of Nazareth.[2]

My King and My Leader, put into my heart so strong a love of You, that I may be eager to follow you everywhere, even to pain and shame. Let the reproach which was flung at Peter be my glory. Let my highest ambition here, let my happiness hereafter be—*Thou also wast with Jesus of Nazareth.*

---

1   Wisdom 23.   2   Matt. 26.

II. To Whom Does He Come?

I see the King standing on a grassy plain near Jerusalem, surrounded by those who believe in Him and love Him. He is fair and beautiful, and the hearts of His servants go out to Him as He stands there in their midst, on the green grass with the wild flowers at His feet. I see Him calling a certain number, a *few* to be His personal followers, His intimate companions, His friends. He chooses them here and there; He calls them by their names one by one. Shall I say to my infinite surprise—shall I say to my extreme confusion—shall I say to my intense joy, I hear my own name called!

I see these so called stepping forth from the ranks and forming a little inner circle round Him—His personal companions, His *friends. I will not now call you servants, but friends.*[1] Such a call is His free gift. He is Master of His gifts and He dispenses them as He chooses. He binds all men by the law of His commandments: He invites a few to the following of His counsels—*I am of that few.* Some souls He designs for great gifts, others for greater, others again for greatest—*I am elected to the greatest.*

---

1   John 25.

Well may I cast down my eyes; well may I thank Him that He does not go by goodness or by fitness, but by His own glorious freedom of choice.

> O Gift of gifts, O gracious call,
>   My God, how can it be,
> That Thou Who hast discerning love
>   Shouldst give that gift *to me!*
>
> How many hearts Thou might'st have had
>   More innocent than mine,
> How many souls more worthy far
>   Of that sweet touch of Thine.
>
> Ah, grace! into unlikeliest hearts
>   It is Thy boast to come,
> The glory of Thy light to find
>   In darkest spots a home.
>
> Thy choice, O God of goodness! then
>   I lovingly adore;
> O give me grace to keep Thy grace
>   And grace to merit more.

Quid retribuam? What shall I give Him? Surely that for which He is looking—the correspondence befitting such a vocation. By my profession I am called to the *special* praise, reverence, and service of God. I must see that He gets this from me. Like a courtier living in the palace, always in the immediate presence of royalty, there must be in my praise, reverence, and service, a delicacy, an assiduity, an exactitude, a generosity not called for from those outside. Mine is a service *more nearly observed* and to be more gloriously requited.

God looks to Religious as to those with whom He may solace Himself. Repelled by the generality of men, He turns to them—*to open Himself* to them. Therefore no minimizing for me, no paring down of a service, which when I have done my best, He must use all His condescension to accept.

But there are degrees of devotedness even in the *corps d' élite*. There are those who are content to fulfil their engagements, to do their own work, to keep in view the movements of their own division. But as to the whole army, to the general interests, to following the King closely—this has no attraction for them— they are not *eminent*.

And there are those whose one desire is to follow their King as closely as possible. Where the battle is thickest—where the blows are hardest—where the marches are longest—and the burdens heaviest— there *they* will be *because He is there*. Mortifications that are not necessary, pain, and injuries, and ignominy are their choice because they were His.

"Always to do *my very best* for Him—All that I can possibly do I will do for Him." This is the cry of their hearts. It shall be my cry. He is a King to live for—a King to die for—a King to Whom it should be a joy to sacrifice personal interest, convenience, comfort, health, strength, time, talents, life itself. Loyalty is a Catholic instinct. In the great Rebellion the persecuted English Catholics brought to the royal cause all the resources that the penal laws had left them. Their plate was melted down, their houses were turned into strongholds for the king. So let it be with all that is mine. Let me gather it all together and lay it at the feet of my King. All is little enough for such a one as He.

Let me do all that lies in me, to make my Congregation a stronghold in His cause. This it will be if His principles reign supreme, if His service is the thought paramount in every heart—not those around me, certainly not *me*, for the first and foremost consideration, but everywhere and always *the King*— His interests, His glory, His greater service.

> For oh, what is the single end
> Of this life's mortal span,
> Except to glorify the God
> Who for our sakes was man?

Thy Kingdom come!—in my own heart first, and then in every heart that I can influence, in those near and dear to me, in those entrusted to me more than all.

My own heart first. Yes, for all strong, lasting influence for good must spring from the interior spirit. It must come of personal devotion to You, of close union with Your Sacred Heart. That Heart must win me to detachment from comforts and convenience, to detachment from honour and reputation, to detachment from self in all its forms if I am to follow my Lord closely, and win souls for Him.

I see Him holding out His hands and saying to me: *Will you come?* Asking for help, asking for personal service, personal devotedness, personal sacrifice— such as He has given to me. *Will you come?* Will you be content with My food, with My cup, with My clothing, content to share My labours and privations, content this coming year with My food—the Will of My Father, with My cup—suffering, with My livery—humiliations and reproaches. *Will you come?* Can I hesitate?

O Sovereign and true Leader, I fall on my knees before You. I am not worthy, I am most unworthy of Your call. But take me as I am. I give myself up into

Your hands. *I will follow Thee whithersoever Thou goest.*[1]
*In what place soever Thou shalt be, my Lord King, either in
death or in life, there will Thy servant be.*[2]

Humility

How St. Francis Borgia prized his vocation!
Perhaps the humility and gratitude of that humble
heart may find its way into mine, if I use his words and
ask to feel as he felt:

"O my Lord, in Whom alone I put my trust, what
is there in me that Thou shouldst look upon me?
What hast Thou found in me, that Thou shouldst
call me to form one of the Company of Thy chosen
servants! For they ought to be valiant, and I am a
coward; they ought to be despisers of the world, and
I am a slave to its opinion; they ought to be haters of
themselves, and I am full of self-love. What then, didst
Thou find in me? Perhaps Thou didst perceive me to
be bolder than others in disobeying Thy commands,
more indifferent to Thy glory, more wedded to my
own interests. Surely, if Thou didst seek these things,
Thou didst find them in me."

---

1   Luke 9.   2   2 Kings 15.

Thy choice, O God of Goodness! then
    I lovingly adore,
Oh, give me grace to keep Thy grace,
    And grace to merit more.

Contrition

In return for all Your favour, my God, You do not ask much, but You do ask for faithfulness. And I have been so unfaithful. There has been so little alacrity in Your service, so much self-seeking, so many short-comings every way.

Yet I know You will not have me to be discouraged. I know You are ready to take us up at any time. Forgive me all there is to forgive—You know, my God, what that means. Could I ask it of any other than You?

III. Why Does He Come?

He comes to fire my heart with the loyal love of Him, with the devotion to His Person on which the fervour of my service depends. He comes to be near me, to put Himself within my reach, to unite Himself intimately to me, that so I may be able to appreciate His character, to learn His ways, *to know Him*. Not to know Him is darkness and death. To know Him is light and life eternal. *This is eternal life, to know Thee,*

the only true God and Jesus Christ, Whom Thou hast sent![1]
He is the Model on the Mount upon which all the
elect are to be formed. The knowledge of Him is the
condition in the order of God's Providence for carrying
out His mission in the world.

What God required in the Apostles was not that
they should be learned men or able men, but that
they should know His Son. St. Peter, too, required
it when he proposed another to fill the place of Judas.
*Of these men who have companied with us, all the time that
the Lord Jesus came in and went out amongst us, . . . one of
these must be made a witness with us.*[2] The same personal
knowledge was given to St. Paul, revealed to him by
our Lord Himself. The same is required in all those
who by their vocation are chosen to carry on the work
of Jesus Christ. It is the condition necessary to success.
It is the training the soldiers must go through before
they can be let loose upon the enemy. An instrument,
to be efficient, must be united to the main agent; we
must be united to our Lord, we must study Him, we
must be like Him in His character, in His ways, in
His likings and dislikings, in His methods, in His
principles, if we are to influence others as He did. He

1　John 17.　　2　Acts 1.

drew all to Him, that He might draw all to God. We must draw all to God by giving them Jesus Christ.

Personal devotion to Him, familiarity with Him, is then an obligation for us. It must be the fruit of study and of prayer. We say of those whom we love, and with whom we are familiarly acquainted, "He would say this, he would act in this way, this reminds me of him, this is like him." So must we come to know Christ our Lord, that we may conform ourselves to Him and bring out His characteristics, some in one way, some in another. This is the secret of finding an easy way into the hearts of all. Those who have this strong, personal devotion to our Lord, have a tact, an address, a facility of approach denied to others. For those who know Him best, love Him most, and are most blessed by Him. They are most near Him and like Him here, to be most near Him and like Him by-and-bye.

This personal devotion to our Lord is the one thing needed by many souls to make them all that God wants, and all that they require to be most useful in His service.

If this be true, O Lord, and I know that it is true, then it is plain why You are coming to me. I shall have much to talk to You about, much to ask, and much to obtain from Your Heart.

Hope and Desire

WHO COMES?

> The Word made Flesh for me,
> The Lord Who died for me,
> The Love made Food for me,
>   He comes!

TO WHOM DOES HE COME?

> To one redeemed by Him,
> To one allied with Him,
> To one who longs for Him,
>   He comes!

WHY DOES HE COME?

> To reign upon His Throne,
> To reign *supreme alone*,
> To make me all His own,
>   He comes!

(AFTER COMMUNION)

Adoration

Now therefore your King is here, Whom you have chosen and desired.[1]

O King, live for ever![2]

I will extol Thee, O God, my King.[3]

Thou alone art my King and my God,[4] *the blessed and only mighty, the King of kings, and Lord of lords,*[5] *my King Who is in His sanctuary.*[6]

Sing praises to our God, sing ye, sing praises to our King, sing ye.[7]

For this is God, our God unto eternity, and for ever and ever; He shall rule for evermore.[8]

Thanksgiving

O bless our God and make the voice of His praise to be heard.[9]

I will cry to God, the most High, to God Who hath done good to me.[10]

1	I Kings 12.	2	Daniel 6.	3	Psalm 144.
4	Psalm 40.	5	I Timothy 6.	6	Psalm 67.
7	Psalm 46.	8	Psalm 47.	9	Psalm 45.
10	Psalm 56.				

Bless the Lord, all ye servants of the Lord, who stand in the house of the Lord, in the courts of the house of our God.[1]

Oh, magnify the Lord with me, and let us extol His name together.[2]

Blessed be the Lord, for He hath shown His wonderful mercy to me.[3]

Let them say so that have been redeemed by the Lord, whom He hath redeemed from the hand of the enemy and gathered out of the countries.[4]

Oh, how hast Thou magnified Thy mercy, O God.[5]

What shall I render to the Lord for all that He hath rendered to me?[6]

Offer to God the sacrifice of praise and pay thy vows to the most High.[7]

I will pay my vows to the Lord in the courts of the house of the Lord, in the midst of thee, O Jerusalem.[8]

Let all Thy works, O Lord, praise Thee, and let all Thy saints bless Thee.[9]

1	Psalm 133.	2	Psalm 33.	3	Psalm 33.
4	Psalm 106.	5	Psalm 35.	6	Psalm 115.
7	Psalm 49.	8	Psalm 115.	9	Psalm 144.

Praise the Lord, O my soul, in my life I will praise the Lord, I will sing to my God as long as I shall be.[1]

What have I in Heaven, but Thee, and besides Thee what do I desire upon earth, Thou art the God of my heart, and the God that is my portion for ever.[2]

O Lord, my God, I will give praise to Thee for ever and ever.[3]

Love

Fear not, for I have redeemed thee and called thee by thy name: thou art Mine.[4]

Yes, I am Yours, my God, Yours wholly, Yours only. I know that if it depended on Your Will alone, my perseverance and salvation would be assured. But there is my own treacherous, inconstant will ever ready to play me false. On what rock can I anchor it, what is there that will secure it against its own instability? One thing only, a strong personal love of Him Whom You have given me for my Redeemer and Saviour.

Of all motives a personal love of Jesus is the strongest and lasts the longest. Others lose their force. The love of God in a vague sort of a way will not stand the test of

1   Psalm 145.   2   Psalm 72.   3   Psalm 29.
4   Isaias 43.

time and trial; temptation comes and those who have relied on it fall away. But those who cling to our Lord with a deep personal love remain steadfast to the end.

That this love may be possible, I must believe firmly in His personal love of me. I am not to say, "Of course our Lord can love this one or that, but I cannot see what He can find to love in me." My seeing has nothing to do with it. I am to believe it heartily, like all other mysteries. He does love me and He wants my love.

Nor must I say, "My heart is cold and hard. He cannot care for love such as mine." Our Lord wants *my* love, such as it is, such as I can give Him. No two hearts give Him the same kind of love. He does not ask me to give Him any one else's love, but my own. He wants of each what each can give. And so He asks of me a love which only my heart can give, a love which if I refuse Him He will never have.

O Lord and Master, how can I refuse what is Yours by every conceivable claim? How can I help bringing to You with joy the little I have to give? Take, O Lord, take all.

O Sovereign and true Leader, O Christ my King, I kneel before You here like a vassal in the old feudal times to take my oath of fealty. I place my joined hands within the wounded hands and renew the dear vows of my Profession. And I bring up to You all that depend on me to show You homage and allegiance. All the powers of my soul, all the senses of my body, all the affections of my heart—I offer them all to You.

Sume et suscipe—Take, take all, O Lord!

O ye Angels... (page 63).

Petition

He sent from on high and took me and drew me out of many waters. He delivered me from my most mighty enemy, and from them that hated me, for they were too strong for me. And He brought me forth into a large place, He delivered me because I pleased Him.[1]

Therefore will I give thanks to Thee, O Lord, and will sing to Thy name.[2]

My God, keep ever fresh in my heart the thanksgiving with which it gave itself to You on the day You called me from the world into Religion, on the day You clothed me with Your livery, on the day You received my vows. As long as that thanksgiving is there, my vocation is safe. At least I was in earnest then. At my Profession I chose You, I forsook all things for You. It was not much, but like Peter I could say it was *all things;* it was all I had, and if it had been

---

1   2 Kings 22.   2   2 Kings 22.

a thousand times more I would gladly have left it to follow You, O Lord. All I had I gave You—body and soul, and mind, and heart, and will, that I might be all Yours and live only for You and for Your service. Has there been rapine in the holocaust? Have I broken my faith with You, my God? Oh, give me grace to be always what I was then, in my desires, in self-surrender, in the sincerity of my oblation. *Confirm, O Lord, what Thou hast wrought in us.*[1] *Renew our days as from the beginning.*[2]

O God, Who called me then and gave me grace to begin, give me now more abundant grace to perfect my offering and make my election sure.

I commend to You all whom You have loved with me and sought out and gathered together with me into the same religious family, all who are under the same roof with me. You have Your designs on all and on each. I offer them each and all to You. Because of their merits, because of their company in which I hope to be found at my death, have mercy on me. You have numbered me with Your chosen ones in this life, number me with them in the life to come. Say to me at Judgment: *Thou art one of them.*[3] Let it be said to each

---

1   Psalm 67.   2   Lament. 5.   3   Mark 14.

of our superiors as to St. Paul: *God hath given thee all them that sail with thee. . . . And so it came to pass that every soul got safe to land.*[1]

Oblation (page 65).

(BEFORE OR AFTER)

Litany for Holy Communion

Lord have mercy on us.
Christ have mercy on us.
Lord have mercy on us.
Christ hear us.
Christ graciously hear us.
God the Father of Heaven,
God the Son, Redeemer of the world,
God the Holy Ghost,
Holy Trinity one God,
Jesus, living Bread Which came down from Heaven,[2]
Jesus, Bread from Heaven giving life to the world,[3]
Hidden God and Saviour,[4]
My Lord and my God,[5]
Who hast loved us with an everlasting love,[6]
Whose delights are to be with the children of men,[7]

Have mercy on us.

---

1   Acts 27. 2   John 6. 3   John 6.
4   Isaias 45. 5   John 20. 6   Jerem. 31.
7   Prov. 8.

Who hast given Thy flesh for the life of the world,[1]

Who dost invite all to come to Thee,[2]

Who dost promise eternal life to those who receive Thee,[3]

Who with desire dost desire to eat this Pasch with us,[4]

Who art ever ready to receive and welcome us,

Who dost stand at our door knocking,[5]

Who hast said that if we will open to Thee the door,
    Thou wilt come in and sup with us,[6]

Who dost receive us into Thy arms and bless us with
    the little children,

Who dost suffer us to sit at Thy feet with Magdalen,

Who dost invite us to lean on Thy bosom with the
    beloved Disciple,

Who hast not left us orphans,[7]

Most dear Sacrament,

Sacrament of love,

Sacrament of sweetness,

Life-giving Sacrament,

Sacrament of strength,

My God and my all,

Have mercy on us.

---

1   John 6.   2   Matt. 11.   3   John 6.

4   Luke 22.   5   Apoc. 3.   6   Apoc. 3.

7   John 14.

That our hearts may pant after Thee as the hart after
the fountains of water,[1]

That Thou wouldst manifest Thyself to us as to the
two disciples in the breaking of bread,[2]

That we may know Thy voice like Magdalen,

That with a lively faith we may confess with the
beloved Disciple—"It is the Lord,"[3]

That Thou wouldst bless us who have not seen and
have believed,[4]

That we may love Thee in the Blessed Sacrament
with our whole heart, with our whole soul, with all
our mind, and with all our strength,[5]

That the fruit of each Communion may be fresh love,

That our one desire may be to love Thee and to do
Thy will,

That we may ever remain in Thy love,[6]

That Thou wouldst teach us how to receive and
welcome Thee,

That Thou wouldst teach us to pray, and Thyself
pray within us,[7]

That with Thee every virtue may come into our souls,

Have mercy on us.

---

1   Psalm 41.   2   Luke 24.   3   John 21.
4   John 20.   5   Mark 12.   6   John 15.
7   Luke 11.

That through this day Thou wouldst keep us closely
   united to Thee,

Jesus, Lover of Poverty, Who hadst not where to lay
   Thy Head, let me follow Thee in perfect poverty,[1]

Jesus, Lover of Chastity, Who feedest among the
   lilies, let me follow Thee in perfect chastity,[2]

Jesus, Lover of Obedience, obedient even unto death,
   let me follow Thee in perfect obedience,[3]

That Thou wouldst give us grace to persevere to the end,[4]

That Thou wouldst then be our support and Viaticum,

That with Thee and leaning on Thee we may safely
   pass through all dangers,

That our last act may be one of perfect love, and our last
   breath a long deep sigh to be in our Father's House,

That Thy sweet Face may smile upon us when we
   appear before Thee,

That our banishment from Thee, dearest Lord, may
   not be very long,

That when the time is come, we may fly up from our
   prison to Thee and in Thy Sacred Heart find our
   rest for ever,

Have mercy on us.

---

1   Matt. 8.   2   Cant. 2.   3   Philipp. 2.
4   Matt. 10.

Lamb of God, Who takest away the sins of the world,
  Spare us, O Lord.
Lamb of God, Who takest away the sins of the world,
  Graciously hear us.
Lamb of God, Who takest away the sins of the world,
  Have mercy on us.

  V. Stay with us, Lord, because it is towards evening.
  R. And the day is now far spent.[1]

Let us pray.

We come to Thee, dear Lord, with the Apostles, saying, *Increase our faith.*[2] Give us a strong and lively faith in the mystery of Thy real Presence in the midst of us. Give us the splendid faith of the centurion, which drew from Thee such praise. Give us the faith of the beloved Disciple to know Thee in the dark and say, *It is the Lord!*[3] Give us the faith of Martha to confess, *Thou art Christ the Son of the living God.*[4] Give us the faith of Magdalen to fall at Thy feet crying, *Rabboni, Master.*[5] Give us the faith of all Thy Saints, to whom the Blessed Sacrament has been Heaven begun on earth. In every Communion increase our faith; for with faith—love and humility, and reverence and all good, will come into our souls.

  Dearest Lord, *increase our faith.*

---

1 Luke 24.   2 Luke 17.   3 John 21.
4 John 11.   5 John 20.

Communion Beads

On the cross, the Prayer of St. Ignatius.

ANIMA CHRISTI

Soul of Christ, sanctify me;
Body of Christ, save me;
Blood of Christ, inebriate me;
Water out of the side of Christ, wash me;
Passion of Christ, strengthen me.
O good Jesus, hear me,
Within Thy wounds hide me;
Never let me be separated from Thee;
From the malignant enemy defend me.
At the hour of my death call me
And bid me come to Thee,
That with Thy saints I may praise Thee
For all eternity.

(300 days' Indulgence.)

On the large beads, Our Father.

On the small beads, Hail, Mary, full of grace, the Lord is with thee, blessed art thou amongst women, and blessed is the fruit of thy womb, Jesus, *Whom thou didst receive so worthily.* Holy Mary, Mother of God, pray for us sinners *that we may receive Him worthily,* now, and at the hour of our death. Amen.

Three decades.

Let us pray.

O God, Who in this wonderful Sacrament hast left us a memorial of Thy passion, grant us, we beseech Thee, so to reverence the sacred mysteries of Thy body and blood, that we may ever find in ourselves the fruit of Thy redemption. Who livest, &c.

Adoro Te Devote

O Hidden God, devoutly unto Thee
    Bends my adoring knee.
With lowly semblances from sight concealed,
    To faith alone revealed.
Fain would my heart transpierce the mystery,
But fails and faints away and yields itself to Thee.

Vision and taste and touch forsake us here,
    Nor tells us Thou art near.
The ear alone we safely trust, and turn
    In faith from Thee to learn.
What God's own Son hath spoken is my creed:
No truer word than His, Who is the Truth indeed.

When to the Cross Thy sacred limbs were nailed,
    Only the God was veiled;
But on the altar here Thy manhood too
    Lies hidden from our view.
Both I believe, though neither can I see,
And with the dying thief I cry, "Remember me."

I cannot see those Wounds now glorified
    In hands and feet and side;
Yet upon Thee, with Thomas, do I call:
    My Lord, my God, my All.
Increase my faith, fix all my hopes on Thee,
And bind my heart to Thine in deathless charity.

O dear memorial of the death of Christ
    For sinners sacrificed,
O Bread that art alive and givest life
    In this our mortal strife,
Grant that my soul may live upon this food
And find in Thee its sweetest, sole abiding good.

For me, dear Pelican, Thy bosom bled,
    For me Thy Blood was shed.
Stained and polluted though my life has been,
    That Blood can make me clean—
That Blood whereof one precious drop could win
Abundant pardon for a thousand worlds of sin.

O Jesu, Whom by faith I now descry
    Shrouded from mortal eye;
When wilt Thou slake the thirsting of my heart
    To see Thee as Thou art,
Face unto face in all Thy glad array,
'Tranced with the glory of that everlasting day.

—George Tyrrell , S.J.

Additional titles available from

ST. AUGUSTINE ACADEMY PRESS
Books for the Traditional Catholic

TITLES BY MOTHER MARY LOYOLA:

Blessed are they that Mourn
Confession and Communion
Coram Sanctissimo (Before the Most Holy)
First Communion
First Confession
Forgive us our Trespasses
Hail! Full of Grace
Heavenwards
Holy Mass/How to Help the Sick and Dying
Home for Good
Jesus of Nazareth: The Story of His Life Written for Children
The Child of God: What comes of our Baptism
The Children's Charter
The Little Children's Prayer Book
The Soldier of Christ: Talks before Confirmation
Trust
Welcome! Holy Communion Before and After

TITLES BY FATHER LASANCE:

The Catholic Girl's Guide
The Young Man's Guide

TALES OF THE SAINTS:

A Child's Book of Saints by William Canton
A Child's Book of Warriors by William Canton
Legends & Stories of Italy by Amy Steedman
Mary, Help of Christians by Rev. Bonaventure Hammer
The Book of Saints and Heroes by Leonora Lang
Saint Patrick: Apostle of Ireland
The Story of St. Elizabeth of Hungary by William Canton

Check our Website for more:
www.staugustineacademypress.com